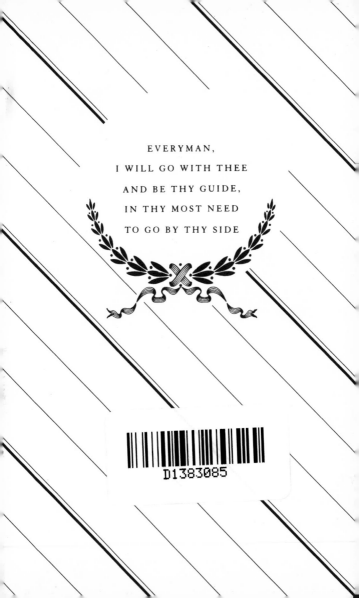

EVERYMAN,
I WILL GO WITH THEE
AND BE THY GUIDE,
IN THY MOST NEED
TO GO BY THY SIDE

EVERYMAN'S LIBRARY
POCKET POETS

RILKE

············

POEMS

EVERYMAN'S LIBRARY
POCKET POETS

This selection by Peter Washington first published in
Everyman's Library, 1996
Translations by J. B. Leishman, and J. B. Leishman and Stephen Spender
© The Hogarth Press, 1960, 1964
Translation of the French Poems Copyright © 1979, 1982, 1984, 1986 by
A. Poulin, Jr. Reprinted by arrangement with Graywolf Press.
Translation of *Letters to a Young Poet* © Reginald Snell, 1945. Reprinted by
permission of Quartet Books Limited.

ISBN 1-85715-730-3

A CIP catalogue record for this book is available from the British Library

Published by David Campbell Publishers Ltd.,
79 Berwick Street, London W1V 3PF

Distributed by Random House (UK) Ltd.,
20 Vauxhall Bridge Road, London SW1V 2SA

Typography by Peter B. Willberg

Typeset by AccComputing, Castle Cary, Somerset

Printed and bound in Germany by
Mohndruck Graphische Betriebe GmbH, Gütersloh

CONTENTS

From SONNETS TO ORPHEUS

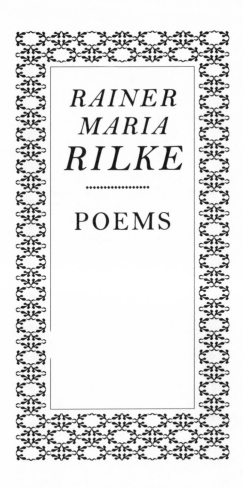

RAINER MARIA RILKE

······················

POEMS

To Monique and Blaise Briod

And by your fire and by lamplight
these big pages will become familiar;
if understanding tires you a bit,
simply hold them to the light
to gild them at its pleasure.
These big pages love to be quiet:
So much silence has collaborated here.

From
THE BOOK OF IMAGES

TRANSLATED BY J. B. LEISHMAN

THE BOY

I'd like, above all, to be one of those
who drive with wild black horses through the night,
torches like hair uplifted in affright
when the great wind of their wild hunting blows.
I'd like to stand in front as in a boat,
tall, like a long floating flag unrolled.
And dark, but with a helmet made of gold,
restlessly flashing. And behind to ride
ten other looming figures side by side,
with helmets matching mine for changefulness,
now clear as glass, now old and lustreless.
And one to stand by me and blow us space
with the brass trumpet that can blaze and blare,
blowing a black solitude through which we tear
like dreams that speed too fast to leave a trace.
Houses behind us fall upon their knees,
alleys cringe crookedly before our train,
squares break in flight: we summon and we seize:
we ride, and our great horses rush like rain.

CHILDHOOD

The school's long stream of time and tediousness
winds slowly on, through torpor, through dismay.
O loneliness, O time that creeps away . . .
Then out at last: the streets ring loud and gay,
and in the big white squares the fountains play,
and in the parks the world seems measureless. –
And to pass through it all in children's dress,
with others, but quite otherwise than they: –
O wondrous time, O time that fleets away,
O loneliness!

And out into it all to gaze and gaze:
men, women, women, men in blacks and greys,
and children, brightly dressed, but differently;
and here a house, and there a dog, maybe,
and fear and trust changing in subtle ways: –
O grief uncaused, O dream, O dark amaze,
O still-unsounded sea!

And then with bat and ball and hoop to playing
in parks where the bright colours softly fade,
brushing against the grown-ups without staying
when ball or hoop their alien walks invade;
but when the twilight comes, with little, swaying
footsteps going home with unrejected aid: –

O thoughts that fade into the darkness, straying
alone, afraid!

And hours on end by the grey pond-side kneeling
with little sailing-boat and elbows bare;
forgetting it, because one like it's stealing
below the ripples, but with sails more fair;
and, having still to spare, to share some feeling
with the small sinking face caught sight of there: –
Childhood! Winged likenesses half-guessed at,
        wheeling,
oh, where, oh, where?

THE LAST SUPPER

Amazed, bewildered, they are gathered round him,
whose pondered resolution comes to rest,
withdrawing him from all the ties that bound him –
a stranger gliding by with thoughts unguessed.
He feels that former loneliness draw near
in which the deep command was comprehended;
again the olive slope shall be ascended,
and those that love him shall depart in fear.

To the last meal of all they've been invited;
and (as a shot will scare some new-alighted
flock from the wheat) their feeding hands, affrighted
from the dealt portions by his prophecy,
fly up to him and flutter in despair
round the round table to escape. But he,
like the still twilight hour, is everywhere.

AUTUMN DAY

Lord, it is time. The summer was so great.
Impose upon the sundials now your shadows
and round the meadows let the winds rotate.

Command the last fruits to incarnadine;
vouchsafe, to urge them on into completeness,
yet two more south-like days; and that last sweetness,
inveigle it into the heavy vine.

He'll not build now, who has no house awaiting.
Who's now alone, for long will so remain:
sit late, read, write long letters, and again
return to restlessly perambulating
the adventures of parks when leaves downrain.

AUTUMN

The leaves are falling, falling as from far,
as though above were withering farthest gardens;
they fall with a denying attitude.

And night by night, down into solitude,
the heavy earth falls far from every star.

We are all falling. This hand's falling too –
all have this falling-sickness none withstands.

And yet there's One whose gently-holding hands
this universal falling can't fall through.

THE ANGELS

They all have mouths so tired, tired
and lucent souls without a seam.
And something guiltily desired
goes sometimes fluttering through their dream.

All so resemblingly reposing
there in God's gardens silently,
like many pauses interposing
within his might and melody.

Save that when each with wings engages
the waiting air, a wind begins
as strong as though beyond the ages
God's sculptor-fingers turned the pages
in the dark book of origins.

From NEW POEMS

TRANSLATED BY J. B. LEISHMAN

EARLY APOLLO

As framing boughs, still leafless, can exhibit
a morning that's already all in Spring,
there's nothing in his head that could prohibit
the splendour of all poems from centring

upon us with an almost fatal shining;
for in his gaze as yet no shadow plays,
his temples are too cool for laurel's twining,
and from his eyebrows not till later days

will that tall-stemmed rose garden be uplifting,
and loosened petals, one by one, be drifting
along the tremors of the mouth below,

as yet still silent, sparkling and unused,
just drinking something with its smile, as though
its singing were being gradually infused.

THE POET'S DEATH

He lay. His high-propped face could only peer
in pale refusal at the silent cover,
now that the world and all this knowledge of her,
torn from the senses of her lover,
had fallen back to the unfeeling year.

Those who had seen him living saw no trace
of his deep unity with all that passes;
for these, these valleys here, these meadow-grasses,
these streams of running water, *were* his face.

Oh yes, his face was this remotest distance,
that seeks him still and woos him in despair;
and his mere mask, timidly dying there,
tender and open, has no more consistence
than broken fruit corrupting in the air.

ORPHEUS. EURYDICE. HERMES

That was the so unfathomed mine of souls.
And they, like silent veins of silver ore,
were winding through its darkness. Between roots
welled up the blood that flows on to mankind,
like blocks of heavy porphyry in the darkness.
Else there was nothing red.

But there were rocks
and ghostly forests. Bridges over voidness
and that immense, grey, unreflecting pool
that hung above its so far distant bed
like a grey rainy sky above a landscape.
And between meadows, soft and full of patience,
appeared the pale strip of the single pathway,
like a long line of linen laid to bleach.

And on this single pathway they approached.

In front the slender man in the blue mantle,
gazing in dumb impatience straight before him.
His steps devoured the way in mighty chunks
they did not pause to chew; his hands were hanging,
heavy and clenched, out of the falling folds,
no longer conscious of the lightsome lyre,
the lyre which had grown into his left
like twines of rose into a branch of olive.

It seemed as though his senses were divided:
for, while his sight ran like a dog before him,
turned round, came back, and stood, time and again,
distant and waiting, at the path's next turn,
his hearing lagged behind him like a smell.
It seemed to him at times as though it stretched
back to the progress of those other two
who should be following up this whole ascent.
Then once more there was nothing else behind him
but his climb's echo and his mantle's wind.
He, though, assured himself they still were coming;
said it aloud and heard it die away.
They still were coming, only they were two
that trod with fearful lightness. If he durst
but once look back (if only looking back
were not undoing of this whole enterprise
still to be done), he could not fail to see them,
the two light-footers, following him in silence:
The god of faring and of distant message,
the travelling-hood over his shining eyes,
the slender wand held out before his body,
the wings around his ankles lightly beating,
and in his left hand, as entrusted, *her*.

She, so belov'd that from a single lyre
more mourning rose than from all women-mourners, –
that a whole world of mourning rose, wherein

all things were once more present: wood and vale
and road and hamlet, field and stream and beast, –
and that around this world of mourning turned,
even as around the other earth, a sun
and a whole silent heaven full of stars,
a heaven of mourning with disfigured stars: –
she, so beloved.

But hand in hand now with that god she walked,
her paces circumscribed by lengthy shroudings,
uncertain, gentle, and without impatience.
Wrapt in herself, like one whose time is near,
she thought not of the man who went before them,
nor of the road ascending into life.
Wrapt in herself she wandered. And her deadness
was filling her like fullness.
Full as a fruit with sweetness and with darkness
was she with her great death, which was so new
that for the time she could take nothing in.

She had attained a new virginity
and was intangible; her sex had closed
like a young flower at the approach of evening,
and her pale hands had grown so disaccustomed
to being a wife, that even the slim god's
endlessly gentle contact as he led her
disturbed her like a too great intimacy.

Even now she was no longer that blonde woman
who'd sometimes echoed in the poet's poems,
no longer the broad couch's scent and island,
nor yonder man's possession any longer.

She was already loosened like long hair,
and given far and wide like fallen rain,
and dealt out like a manifold supply.

She was already root.
And when, abruptly,
the god had halted her and, with an anguished
outcry, outspoke the words: He has turned round! –
she took in nothing, and said softly: Who?

But in the distance, dark in the bright exit,
someone or other stood, whose countenance
was indistinguishable. Stood and saw
how, on a strip of pathway between meadows,
with sorrow in his look, the god of message
turned silently to go behind the figure
already going back by that same pathway,
its paces circumscribed by lengthy shroudings,
uncertain, gentle, and without impatience.

ROMAN SARCOPHAGI

Why should we too, though, not anticipate
(set down here and assigned our places thus)
that only for a short time rage and hate
and this bewildering will remain in us,

as in the ornate sarcophagus, enclosed
with images of gods, rings, glasses, trappings,
there lay in slowly self-consuming wrappings
something being slowly decomposed –

till swallowed by those unknown mouths at last,
that never speak. (Where bides a brain that may
yet trust the utterance of its thinking to them?)

Then from the ancient aqueducts there passed
eternal water into them one day: –
that mirrors now and moves and sparkles
        through them.

THE PANTHER
JARDIN DES PLANTES, PARIS

His gaze those bars keep passing is so misted
with tiredness, it can take in nothing more.
He feels as though a thousand bars existed,
and no more world beyond them than before.

Those supply-powerful paddings, turning there
in tiniest of circles, well might be
the dance of forces round a centre where
some mighty will stands paralyticly.

Just now and then the pupil's noiseless shutter
is lifted. – Then an image will indart,
down through the limbs' intensive stillness flutter,
and ends its being in the heart.

THE SWAN

This laborious going on and on,
bound and heavy, through the still-to-do is
like the unshaped walking of the swan.

Dying too, that no more hold-providing
by the ground we daily trusted to, is
like his so unconfident subsiding

into waters that receive him gently
and, as though departed and contently,
wave on wave retire from under him;
while he, infinitely still and surely,
ever kinglier and more maturely,
more composedly, condescends to swim.

THE UNICORN

And then the saint looked up, and in surprise
the prayer fell like a helmet from his head:
for softly neared that never-credited
white creature, which, like some unparented,
some helpless hind, beseeches with its eyes.

The ivory framework of the limbs so light
moved like a pair of balances deflected,
there glided through the coat a gleam of white,
and on the forehead, where the beams collected,
stood, like a moon-lit tower, the horn so bright,
at every footstep proudly re-erected.

Its mouth was slightly open, and a trace
of white through the soft down of grey and rose
(whitest of whites) came from the gleaming teeth;
its nostrils panted gently for repose.
Its gaze, though, checked by nothing here beneath,
projecting pictures into space,
brought a blue saga-cycle to a close.

THE GAZELLE
Gazella dorcas

Enchanted thing: however can the chime
of two selected words attain the true
rhyme that, as beckoned, comes and goes in you?
Out of your forehead leaf and lyre climb,

and all you are has been in simile
passing through those love-songs continually
whose words will cover, light as leaves of rose,
the no-more-reader's eyes, which he will close:

only to look upon you: so impelled
as though each limb of yours with leaps were laden,
and held its fire but while the neck upheld

the head in hearkening: as when a maiden
breaks off from bathing in some lonely place,
the forest-lake within her swift-turned face.

THE DOG

Up there's the image of a world which glances
are always re-establishing as true.
At times, though, secretly, a thing advances
and stands beside him when he's squeezing through

that image, he so different, down below;
neither excluded nor incorporate,
and squandering, as in doubt, his true estate
upon that image he forgets, although

he still keeps pushing so persistently
his face into it, almost with beseeching,
so close to comprehension, nearly reaching,
and yet renouncing: for he wouldn't *be*.

PARTING

How I have felt that thing that's called 'to part',
and feel it still: a dark, invincible,
cruel something by which what was joined so well
is once more shown, held out, and torn apart.

In what defenceless gaze at that I've stood,
which, as it, calling to me, let me go,
stayed there, as though it were all womanhood,
yet small and white and nothing more than, oh,

a waving, now already unrelated
to me, a sight, continuing wave, – scarce now
explainable: perhaps a plum-tree bough
some perching cuckoo's hastily vacated.

LADY BEFORE THE MIRROR

At the mirror's surface she'll begin
gently melting, like a spice-assortment
in a sleeping draught, her tired deportment;
and she'll let her smiling drop right in.

And she'll wait until the liquidness
rises from it; then she'll pour her hair
in as well, and, lifting out one bare,
marvellous shoulder from her evening-dress,

quietly drink out her image. Drink,
what a lover would in wild caresses,
tryingly, all mistrust; and never think

of beckoning her maid until she sees
at the mirror's bottom candles, presses,
and a late hour's undissolving lees.

PORTRAIT OF MY FATHER
AS A YOUNG MAN

Dream in the eyes. The brow as in relation
with something distant. Mouth with more than norm
of youth, unsmilingly diffused temptation,
and, placed before the corded decoration
of the slim, gentlemanly uniform,
the sabre-hilt and those two hands, that stay
quiescent, – with no passionate intent.
And hardly to be seen now: as if they
were first to vanish, grasping the unscanned.
And all the rest in self-envelopment
and quenched as if we didn't understand
and deeply, from its very depth, opaque.

You swiftly fading daguerrotype I take
in my more gradually fading hand.

REQUIEM

TRANSLATED BY J. B. LEISHMAN

FOR A FRIEND

I have my dead, and I would let them go
and be surprised to see them all so cheerful,
so soon at home in being-dead, so right,
so unlike their repute. You, you alone,
return; brush past me, move about, persist
in knocking something that vibratingly
betrays you. Oh, don't take from me what I
am slowly learning. I'm right; you're mistaken,
if you're disturbed into a home-sick longing
for something here. We transmute it all;
it's not here, we reflect it from ourselves,
from our own being, as soon as we perceive it.

    I thought you'd got much further. It confounds me
that *you* should thus mistake and come, who passed
all other women so in transmutation.
That we were frightened when you died, or, rather,
that your strong death made a dark interruption,
tearing the till-then from the ever-since:
that is our business: to set that in order
will be the work that everything provides us.
But that you too were frightened, even now
are frightened, now, when fright has lost its meaning,
that you are losing some of your eternity,
even a little, to step in here, friend, here,
where nothing yet exists; that in the All,

for the first time distracted and half-hearted,
you did not grasp the infinite ascension
as once you grasped each single thing on earth;
that from the orbit that already held you
the gravitation of some mute unrest
should drag you down to measurable time:
this often wakes me like an entering thief.
If I could say you merely deign to come
from magnanimity, from superabundance,
because you are so sure, so self-possessed,
that you can wander like a child, not frightened
of places where ther're things that happen to one –
but no, you're asking. And that penetrates
right to the bone and rattles like a saw.
Reproach, such as you might bear as a spirit,
bear against me when I withdraw myself
at night into my lungs, into my bowels,
into the last poor chamber of my heart,
such a reproach would not be half so cruel
as this mute asking. What is it you ask?

    Say, shall I travel? Have you left somewhere
a thing behind you, that torments itself
with trying to reach you? Travel to a country
you never saw, although it was as closely
akin to you as one half of your senses?

    I'll voyage on its rivers, set my foot
upon its soil and ask about old customs,

stand talking with the women in their doorways
and pay attention when they call their children.
I will observe how they take on the landscape
outside there in the course of the old labour
of field and meadow; will express a wish
to be presented to the king himself,
and work upon the priests with bribery
to leave me lying before the strongest statue
and then withdraw, shutting the temple doors.
But in conclusion, having learnt so much,
I'll simply watch the animals, that something
of their own way of turning may glide over
into my joints; I'll have a brief existence
within their eyes, that solemnly retain me
and slowly loose me, calmly, without judgement.
I'll make the gardeners repeat by heart
the names of many flowers and so bring back
in pots of lovely proper names a remnant,
a little remnant, of the hundred perfumes.
And I will purchase fruits too, fruits, wherein
that country, sky and all, will re-exist.

   For that was what you understood: full fruits.
You used to set them out in bowls before you
and counterpoise their heaviness with colours.
And women too appeared to you as fruits,
and children too, both of them from within
impelled into the forms of their existence.

And finally you saw yourself as fruit,
lifted yourself out of your clothes and carried
that self before the mirror, let it in
up to your gaze; which remained, large, in front,
and did not say: that's me; no, but: this is.
So uninquiring was your gaze at last,
so unpossessive and so truly poor,
it wanted even you no longer: holy.

That's how I would retain you, as you placed
yourself within the mirror, deep within,
and far from all else. Why come differently?
Why thus revoke yourself? Why are you trying
to make me feel that in those amber beads
around your neck there was still something heavy
with such a heaviness as never lurks
in the beyond of tranquil pictures? Why
does something in your bearing bode misfortune?
What makes you read the contours of your body
like lines upon a hand, and me no longer
able to see them but as destiny?

Come to the candle-light. I'm not afraid
to look upon the dead. When they return
they have a right to hospitality
within our gaze, the same as other things.

Come; we'll remain a little while in silence.
Look at this rose, here on my writing-desk:
is not the light around it just as timid

as that round you? It too should not be here.
It ought to have remained or passed away
out in the garden there, unmixed with me –
it stays, unconcious of my consciousness.

Don't be afraid now if I comprehend:
it's rising in me – oh, I must, I must,
even if it kills me, I must comprehend.
Comprehend, that you're here. I comprehend.
Just as a blind man comprehends a thing,
I feel your fate although I cannot name it.
Let both of us lament that someone took you
out of your mirror. If you still can cry?
No, you can't cry. You long ago transformed
the force and thrust of tears to your ripe gazing,
and were in act of changing every kind
of sap within you to a strong existence
that mounts and circles in blind equipoise.
Then, for the last time, chance got hold of you,
and snatched you back out of your farthest progress,
back to a world where saps will have their way.
Did not snatch all, only a piece at first,
but when reality, from day to day,
so swelled around that piece that it grew heavy,
you needed your whole self; then off you went
and broke yourself in fragments from your law,
laboriously, needing yourself. And then

you took yourself away and from your heart's
warm, night-warm, soil you dug the yet green seeds
your death was going to spring from: your own death,
the death appropriate to your own life.
And then you ate those grains of your own death
like any others, ate them one by one,
and had within yourself an after-taste
of unexpected sweetness, had sweet lips,
you: in your senses sweet within already.

    Let us lament. Do you know how unwilling
and hesitatingly your blood returned,
recalled from an incomparable orbit?
With what confusion it took up again
the tiny circulation of the body?
With what mistrust it entered the placenta,
suddenly tired from the long homeward journey?
You drove it on again, you pushed it forward,
you dragged it to the hearth, as people drag
a herd of animals to sacrifice;
and spite of all desired it to be happy.
And finally you forced it: it was happy,
and ran up and surrendered. You supposed,
being so accustomed to the other measures,
that this was only for a little while;
but now you were in time, and time is long.
And time goes by, and time goes on, and time

is like relapsing after some long illness.

How very short your life, when you compare it
with hours you used to sit in silence, bending
the boundless forces of your boundless future
out of their course to the new germination,
that became fate once more. O painful labour.
Labour beyond all strength. And you performed it
day after day, you dragged yourself along to it
and pulled the lovely woof out of the loom
and wove your threads into another pattern.
And still had spirit for a festival.

For when you'd done you looked for some reward,
like children, when they've drunk a nasty drink
of bitter-sweet tea that may make one better.
You gave your own reward, being still so distant,
even then, from all the rest; and no one there
who could have hit on a reward to please you.
You yourself knew it. You sat up in child-bed,
a mirror there before you, that returned
all that you gave. Now everything was you,
and right in front; within was mere deceit,
the sweet deceit of Everywoman, gladly
putting her jewels on and doing her hair.

And so you died like women long ago,
died in the old warm house, old-fashionedly,
the death of those in child-bed, who are trying

to close themselves again but cannot do it,
because that darkness which they also bore
returns and grows importunate and enters.

　　Ought they not, though, to have gone and hunted up
some mourners for you? Women who will weep
for money, and, if paid sufficiently,
will howl through a whole night when all is still.
Observances! We haven't got enough
observances. All vanishes in talk.
That's why you have to come back, and with me
retrieve omitted mourning. Can you hear me?
I'd like to fling my voice out like a cloth
over the broken fragments of your death
and tug at it till it was all in tatters,
and everything I said was forced to go
clad in the rags of that torn voice and freeze –
if mourning were enough. But I accuse:
not him who thus withdrew you from yourself
(I can't distinguish him, he's like them all),
but in him I accuse all: accuse man.
　　If somewhere deep within me rises up
a having-once-been-child I don't yet know,
perhaps the purest childness of my childhood:
I will not know it. Without looking at it
or asking, I will make an angel of it,

and hurl that angel to the foremost rank
of crying angels that remembrance God.

For now too long this suffering has lasted,
and none can stand it; it's too hard for us,
this tortuous suffering caused by spurious love,
which, building on prescription like a habit,
calls itself just and battens on injustice.
Where is the man who justly may possess?
Who can possess what cannot hold itself
but only now and then blissfully catches
and flings itself on like a child a ball?
As little as the admiral can retain
the Nikê poised upon his vessel's prow
when the mysterious lightness of her godhead
has caught her up into the limpid sea-wind,
can one of us call back to him the woman
who, seeing us no longer, takes her way
along some narrow strip of her existence,
as though a miracle, without mischance –
unless his calling and delight were guilt.

For this is guilt, if anything be guilt,
not to enlarge the freedom of a love
with all the freedom in one's own possession.
All we can offer where we love is this:
to loose each other; for to hold each other
comes easy to us and requires no learning.

* * *

Are you still there? Still hiding in some corner? –
You knew so much of all that I've been saying,
and could so much too, for you passed through life
open to all things, like a breaking day.
Women suffer: loving means being lonely,
and artists feel at times within their work
the need, where most they love, for transmutation.
You began both; and both exist in *that*
which fame, detaching it from you, disfigures.
Oh, you were far beyond all fame. Were in-
conspicuous; had gently taken in
your beauty as a gala flag's intaken
on the grey morning of a working-day,
and wanted nothing but a lengthy work –
which is not done; in spite of all, not done.

    If you're still there, if somewhere in this darkness
there's still a spot where your perceptive spirit's
vibrating on the shallow waves of sound
a lonely voice within a lonely night
starts in the air-stream of a lofty room:
hear me and help me. Look, without knowing when,
we keep on slipping backwards from our progress
into some unintended thing, and there
we get ourselves involved as in a dream,
and there at last we die without awakening.

No one's got further. Anyone who's lifted
the level of his blood to some long work
may find he's holding it aloft no longer
and that it's worthlessly obeying its weight.
For somewhere there's an old hostility
between our human life and greatest work.
May I see into it and it say: help me!

    Do not return. If you can bear it, stay
dead with the dead. The dead are occupied.
But help me, as you may without distraction,
as the most distant sometimes helps: in me.

From POEMS
1906 to 1926

TRANSLATED BY J. B. LEISHMAN

FROM THE POEMS OF COUNT C.W.

Karnak. We'd ridden, dinner quickly done with,
Hélène and I, to get the moonlight view.
The dragoman pulled up: the Avenue, –
the Pylon, ah! I'd never felt so one with

the lunar world! (Are you being magnified
within me, greatness? then beyond control?)
Is travel – seeking? Well, this was a goal.
The watchman at the entrance first supplied

the frightening scale. How lowly seemed his station
beside the gate's unchecked self-exaltation!
And then, for a whole life-time's meditation
did not the Column bring enough and more?

Ruin vindicated it: it would have been
too high for highest roof. It stood and bore
Egyptian night.
                              The following fellaheen

now fell behind us. To get over this
took time, because it almost stopped the heart
to know that such out-standing formed a part
of that same being we died in. – If I had
a son, I'd send him, when our only care

is finding truth to live by: 'Charles, it's there, –
walk through the Pylon, stand and look, my lad.'

Why could it not help *us* more helpfully?
That we endured it was enough indeed:
you in your travelling dress, the invalid,
and I the hermit in my theory.

And yet, the mercy! Can you still recall
that lake round which the granite cats were seated?
Mark-stones (of what?). So chained, as by repeated
spells, into that enchanted rectangle

one felt, that had not five been overturned
along one side (you too were overcome),
they would that moment, cattish, stony, dumb,
have held a court of judgement.
                        All discerned
was judgement. Here the ban upon the pond,
there on the margin the giant scarabee,
along the walls the epic history
of monarchs: judgement. And yet, quite beyond

all comprehension, an acquittal too.
As figure after figure there was filled
with the pure moonlight, the relief, outdrilled
in clearest outline, hollow, trough-like, grew

so much receptacle – for nothing less
than what, though never hidden, none could see,
for the world-secret, so essentially
secret, it baffles all secretiveness!

All books keep turning past it: no one ever
read in a book a thing so manifest
(I want a word – how can it be expressed?):
the Immeasurable submitted to the measure

of sacrifice. – Look there, oh, look: what's keeping,
that has not learnt to give itself away?
All things are passing. Help them on their way.
And then your life will not be merely seeping

out through some crack. Remain your whole life long
the conscious giver. Mule and cow, they throng
in close procession to the spot where he,
the god-king, like a stilled child, peaceably

receives and smiles. His mighty sacredness
is never out of breath. He takes and takes:
and yet such mitigation overtakes,
that the papyrus flower by the princess

is often merely clasped, not broken. –
                                        Here

all ways of sacrifice abruptly end,
the Sabbath starts, the long weeks comprehend
its mind no longer. Man and beast appear

to keep at times some gains from the god's eyes.
Profit, though difficult, can be secured;
one tries and tries, the earth can be procured, –
yet who but gives the price gives up the prize.

THE FRUIT

It climbed and climbed from earth invisibly,
and kept its secret in the silent stem,
and turned in the clear blossom into flame,
and then resumed its secrecy.

And through a whole long summer fructified
within that day and night travailing tree,
and felt itself as urging instancy
to meet responding space outside.

And though it now displays so shiningly
that rondure of completed rest anew,
within the rind it sinks resigningly
back to the centre it outgrew.

THE RAISING OF LAZARUS

One had to bear with the majority –
what they wanted was a sign that screamed:
Martha, though, and Mary – he had dreamed
they would be contented just to see
that he *could*. But not a soul believed him:
'Lord, you've come too late,' said all the crowd.
So to peaceful Nature, though it grieved him,
on he went to do the unallowed.
Asked them, eyes half-shut, his body glowing
with anger, 'Where's the grave?' Tormentedly.
And to them it seemed his tears were flowing,
as they thronged behind him, curiously.
As he walked, the thing seemed monstrous to him,
childish, horrible experiment:
then there suddenly went flaming through him
such an all-consuming argument
against their life, their death, their whole collection
of separations made by them alone,
all his body quivered with rejection
as he gave out hoarsely 'Raise the stone'.
Someone shouted that the corpse was stinking
(buried now four days ago) – but He
stood erect, brim-full of that unblinking,
mounting gesture, that so painfully
lifted up his hand (no hand was ever

raised so slowly, so immeasurably),
till it stood there, shining in the gloom.
There it slowly, clawingly contracted:
what if all the dead should be attracted
upwards, through that syphon of a tomb,
where a pallid chrysalidal thing
was writhing up from where it had been lying? –
But it stood alone (no more replying),
and they saw vague, unidentifying
Life compelled to give it harbouring.

ON THE SUNNY ROAD

On the sunny road, within the hollow
cloven tree, that now for generations
has been a trough, inaudibly renewing
a little film of water, I can still my
thirst by letting all that pristine freshness
ripple from my wrists through all my body.
Drinking seems to me too much, too open:
this more patient, more expectant gesture
fills my consciousness with sparkling water.

So, if you came, I could be contented
just to let my hands rest very lightly
either on your shoulder's youthful rounding
or upon your breasts' responsive pressure.

STARS BEHIND OLIVES

Dear love, who fail to read so much aright,
lean back, till in sheer leafage you can see
the places that are stars. It may well be
that earth's not really different from night.

Look how within this self-forgotten bower
the nearest and the nameless interweave:
we are shown this, not merely for an hour
offered what casual visitors receive.

We've not, in all this sad perambulation,
worn out the garden with the pain we brought,
and hours surpassing all our expectation
grope after us and walk with our support.

TO HÖLDERLIN

Lingering, even with intimate things,
is not vouchsafed us; the spirit plunges
from filled to suddenly fillable images; lakes
exist in eternity. Falling is here
fittest. Cascading down out of compassed feeling
into surmised beyond.

You, though, glorious invoker, for you a whole life
    was that
importunate image; when you expressed it,
a line locked up like destiny, even in the gentlest
there lurked a death, which you lighted upon,
    but the god
going before you guided you forth and afar.

Oh, you ranging spirit, you rangingest! Look how
    they all
dwell as at home in cosy poems and make
long stays in narrow comparisons. Participators.
    You only
move like the moon. And below there brightens and
    darkens
your own nocturnal, sacredly startled landscape,
the one you feel in partings. No one
surrendered it more sublimely, gave it more wholly,

dispensably, back to the whole. Such, too,
was your holy play, through the now uncounted years,
with happiness, as though it were not internal,
but lay about unclaimed
on earth's soft turf, left by celestial children.
Oh, what the loftiest long for, you laid, with never a wish,
stone upon stone: it stood. And when it collapsed it left you
unbewildered.

Why, after such an eternal life, do we still
mistrust the terrestrial? Instead of earnestly learning
from fleeting Appearance the feelings
for, oh, what affections, in space?

TO MUSIC
(THE PROPERTY OF FRAU HANNA WOLFF)

Music: breathing of statues. Perhaps:
stillness of pictures. You speech, where speeches
end. You time,
vertically poised on the courses of vanishing hearts.

Feelings for what? Oh, you transformation
of feelings into … audible landscape!
You stranger: Music. Space that's outgrown us,
heart-space. Innermost us, transcendently
surging away from us, – holiest parting,
where what is within surrounds us
as practised horizon, as other
side of the air,
pure,
gigantic,
no longer lived in.

FOR COUNT KARL LANCKOROŃSKI

'No intellect, no ardour is redundant':
to make one through the other more abundant
is what we're for, and some are singled out
for purest victory in that contention:
no signal can escape their tried attention,
their hands are wieldy and their weapons stout.

No sound must be too soft for their detection,
they must perceive that angle of deflection
to which the dial scarcely stirs,
and must, as might be with their eyelids, utter
reply to what the butterflies out-flutter,
and learn to fathom what a flower infers.

No less than others they can be extinguished,
and yet they must (why else were they distinguished?)
feel even with catastrophe some kin,
and, while the rest are helplessly bewailing,
recapture in the strokes of each assailing
the rhythm of some stoniness within.

They must be stationed like a shepherd, keeping
his lonely watch: one might suppose him weeping,
till, coming close, one feels his piercing sight;
and, as for him the speech of stars is clear,
for them must be as intimately near
what climbs in still procession through the night.

In slumber also they continue seers:
from dream and being, from laughter and from tears
a meaning gathers ... which if they can seize,
and kneel to Life and Death in adoration,
another measure for the whole creation
is given us in those right-angled knees.

From FRENCH POEMS

TRANSLATED BY A. POULIN, JR.

TITMOUSE

O you, small heart that winters
out these bitter winter days with us
– tender lantern of life,
you perch on the weeping trees;

I reflect on the fire shining
through your thick-set feathers,
and I, more hidden by the mist,
I'm not afraid to burn out, either.

Does this snow fear tomorrow?
In fact, it hardens in vain;
but we, protected by a flame,
we'll know the pleasure of tomorrow.

*

Let's stay by the lamp and say little;
all we can say isn't worth the avowal
of silence lived; it's like the pit
of a divine hand.
The hand is empty, surely, this hand;
but a hand never opens in vain,
and we're combined by this one.

It isn't ours: we accelerate
slow things. An opening hand
is already action. Let's look
at the life that flows in it.
The one that moves isn't the strongest.
We must admire its tacit harmony,
before power starts to stir.

*

Will I have expressed it before I leave,
this heart that, tormented, consents to be?
Endless astonishment that mastered me,
will I have imitated you up to the end?

But, like a summer day, all else pales
the tender gesture that admires too late;
from our words in bloom, who inhales
the pure fragrance of identity?

And that departing woman,
how can she be made into metaphor?
Her soft ribbon flutters, livelier
than this infatuated line.

*

From THE VALAISIAN QUATRAINS

Landscape stopped halfway
between the earth and sky,
with voices of bronze and water,
ancient and new, tough and tender,

like an offering lifted
toward accepting hands:
lovely completed land,
warm, like bread!

*

Before you can count ten,
all changes: wind takes
the brightness from high
stalks of maize

to throw it on all sides;
it flies, it slides
along a precipice
toward a sister brightness

which, already taken up
in this rough game,
in turn moves herself
toward other altitudes.

And, as if caressed,
dazzled by these games
that maybe gave it shape,
the vast surface rests.

*

Road that turns and plays
along the leaning vineyard,
like a ribbon that we wind
around a summer hat.

Vineyard: hat on the head
that invents the wine.
Wine: blazing comet
promised for next year.

*

The small clematis tumbles
from the hedge that's tangled
with the morning glory watching
for that time to close again.

All along the road they make
bouquets where berries redden.
Is summer over? Already?
It picks autumn as accomplice.

*

After a day of wind,
the night is at ease
in an infinite peace
like a docile lover.

All turns calm, clear. . . .
But on the horizon, tiered,
glowing and gold,
a lovely bas-relief of clouds.

*

Wind that grips this country like a craftsman
who, from the start, has known his material;
finding it hot, he knows what must be done
and grows enthusiastic with his work.

No one could stop this magnificent momentum;
no one could oppose this fiery defiance –
and he is still the one who takes a long step back
to offer his work the bright mirror of space.

*

A beautiful butterfly near
the earth is displaying
the illuminations of its flying
book to an attentive nature.

Another closes on the border
of the flower that we breathe:
this is not the time to read.
And still so many others,

fragile blues scattered,
floating and fluttering
like the blue fragmenting
of a love letter in the wind,

of a torn-up letter
we had just been writing
while its addressee
hesitated at the door.

*

From ORCHARDS

PALM

Palm, soft unmade bed,
where sleeping stars left
wrinkles as they rose
up towards the sky.

Was this bed such
that they are rested,
clear and incandescent,
among the friendly stars
in their eternal swirl?

Oh, the two beds of my hands,
abandoned and cold,
light with the absent load
of those brazen stars.

SUMMER PASSER-BY

Do you see that slowly walking, happy
girl coming down the road, the one we envy?
At some turn in the road she ought to be
greeted by handsome men of days gone by.

Under her parasol, with passive grace,
she exploits the tender alternative:
disappearing briefly in the blinding light,
she gathers the shade of her incandescence.

THE FOUNTAIN

I want just one lesson, and it's yours,
fountain falling back into yourself –
that of risked waters on which depends
this celestial return towards earthly life.

Nothing will serve as example
as much as your multiple murmur:
you, O light column of a temple
that destroys itself by nature.

In your fall, how each jet of water
modulates itself as it ends its dance.
I feel like such a student, imitator
of your innumerable nuance.

But what's more convincing than your singing
is that instant of ecstatic silence when
at night, drawn back by a breath, your own
return passes through your liquid leaping.

INTERIOR PORTRAIT

You don't survive in me
because of memories;
nor are you mine because
of a lovely longing's strength.

What does make you present
is the ardent detour
that a slow tenderness
traces in my blood.

I do not need
to see you appear;
being born sufficed for me
to lose you a little less.

*

A swan swims on the water
surrounded by itself
like a gliding picture;
thus at certain moments
a being that we love
is utter space in motion.

Like this swimming swan,
doubled, it comes closer
on our troubled soul . . .
which to this being adds
the rippling image
of happiness and doubt.

*

All my goodbyes are said. Many separations
slowly shaped me since my infancy.
But I come back again and I begin again;
this fresh return releases my attention.

What's left for me is to replenish it,
and my joy, forever unrepentant
for having loved the things resembling
these absences that make us act.

*

CAT

The show cat: a soul conferring
its slow dream on all those scattered objects,
and in primal consciousness bestowing
itself to a whole unconscious world.

Warm and musky silence imposing
itself on the mutilated muteness
and filling the orphanage of things
with a proud disdain for being caressed. . . .

Among the crystals, fayences, and gilts,
she sleeps with such an integral air
that the plaintive pattern of their cracks
seems signed by magisterial misfortune.

DIVINE DISGRACE

Too unfaithful mouth, my blunt will
shall never speak through you again;
I tried you out, but your breath scrambles
my dictation with all the hazards of the heart.

If there is tenderness, it will be yours alone:
sugary aftertaste, colored saliva,
seducing everything a little, quickly insipid . . .
anything but the honey multiplied in me.

From now on it shall be you, harshness or bitterness
you alone shall ring under numberless blows:
for I am the hammer and you remain the anvil,
but no more iron forged between us!

GROWING OLD

In some summers there is so much fruit,
the peasants decide not to reap any more.
Not having reaped you, oh my days,
my nights, have I let the slow flames
of your lovely produce fall into ashes?

My nights, my days, you have borne so much!
All your branches have retained the gesture
of that long labor you are rising from:
my days, my nights. Oh my rustic friends!

I look for what was so good for you.
Oh my lovely, half-dead trees,
could some equal sweetness still
stroke your leaves, open your calyx?

Ah, no more fruit! But one last time
bloom in fruitless blossoming
without planning, without reckoning,
as uselessly as the powers of millennia.

TO THE MOON

Moon, svelte person,
who makes you pregnant
every month?
And who makes you always
engrossed in your pregnancy
– almost terrestrially?

You attract the blood
of our pubescent virgins.
But what do you mother
twelves times a year?

Shall we raise your light
offspring in ourselves?
Inside me I found a soft
cradle decorated with gilt
which I think suits your taste.

WATER LILY

My whole life is mine, but whoever says so
will deprive me, for it is infinite.
The ripple of water, the shade of the sky
are mine; it is still the same, my life.

No desire opens me: I am full,
I never close myself with refusal –
in the rhythm of my daily soul
I do not desire – I am moved;

by being moved I exert my empire,
making the dreams of night real:
into my body at the bottom of the water
I attract the beyonds of mirrors. . . .

WHAT SURVIVES

Who says that all must vanish?
Who knows, perhaps the flight
of the bird you wound remains,
and perhaps flowers survive
caresses in us, in their ground.

It isn't the gesture that lasts,
but it dresses you again in gold
armor – from breast to knees –
and the battle was so pure
an Angel wears it after you.

TELLING YOU ALL

Telling you all would take too long.
Besides, we read in the Bible
how the good is harmful
and how misfortune is good.

Let's invite something new
by unifying our silences;
if, then and there, we advance,
we'll know it soon enough.

And yet towards evening,
when his memory is persistent,
one belated curiosity
stops him before the mirror.

We don't know if he is frightened.
But he stays, he is engrossed,
and, facing his reflection,
transports himself somewhere else.

FIRE'S REFLECTION

Perhaps it's no more than the fire's reflection
on some piece of gleaming furniture
that the child remembers so much later
like a revelation.

And if in his later life, one day
wounds him like so many others,
it's because he mistook some risk
or other for a promise.

Let's not forget the music, either,
that soon had hauled him
toward absence complicated
by an overflowing heart. . . .

NO ONE SPEAKS OF THEM

No one speaks of them, and yet
they were avid to live;
they were more than the wind
which sometimes decides our fate. . . .

They were charming and pure.

Who can guess their names
erased in cemeteries?
Those simple names of yesteryear
that they preferred

like a flower we prefer.

We love the new so much.
These striplings, certainly,
were newer than need be
to shatter a tomb.

MOMENT BETWEEN MASKS

As long as we stayed in closed rooms
and stiff coats, we were disguised;
but toward the end of winter the carnival
helps us to *play* at disguise for a while.

For soon spring will remove all the masks:
it wants a clear country, an honest garden;
already a fully naked air leans on the basin
where water waits for the shadows of spring.

We'll feel its body, full of sap, stretch,
but have we ever seen its face?
Barely adult, it never takes off
the mask of greenery it completes.

CHILD IN RED

Sometimes she walks through the village in her
    little red dress
all absorbed in restraining herself,
and yet, despite herself, she seems to move
according to the rhythm of her life to come.

She runs a bit, hesitates, stops,
half-turns around . . .
and, all while dreaming, shakes her head
for or against.

Then she dances a few steps
that she invents and forgets,
no doubt finding out that life
moves on too fast.

It's not so much that she steps out
of the small body enclosing her,
but that all she carries in herself
frolics and ferments.

It's this dress that she'll remember
later in a sweet surrender;
when her whole life is full of risks,
the little red dress will always seem right.

WHITE LILY

White lily, just by dint of being
so white – : to come to what?
While reflecting a sigh
from all other colors, it dreams.

The garden scatters a desperate
brilliance around it;
in shade, its white is full
of so many stirring absences . . .

BLANK JOY

She who did not come, wasn't she determined
nonetheless to organize and decorate my heart?
If we had to exist to become the one we love,
what would the heart have to create?

Lovely joy left blank, perhaps you are
the center of all my labors and my loves.
If I've wept for you so much, it's because
I preferred you among so many outlined joys.

NARCISSUS

Encircled by her arms as by a shell,
she hears her being murmur,
while forever he endures
the outrage of his too pure image....

Wistfully following their example,
nature re-enters herself;
contemplating its own sap, the flower
becomes too soft, and the boulder hardens....

It's the return of all desire that enters
toward all life embracing itself from afar....
Where does it fall? Under the dwindling
surface, does it hope to renew a center?

THE FUTURE

The future: time's excuse
to frighten us; too vast
a project, too large a morsel
for the heart's mouth.

Future, who won't wait for you?
Everyone is going there.
It suffices you to deepen
the absence that we are.

EVENING LOVE SONG

Ornamental clouds
compose an evening love song;
a road leaves evasively.
The new moon begins

a new chapter of our nights,
of those frail nights
we stretch out and which mingle
with these black horizontals.

THE WAIT

It is life in slow motion,
it's the heart in reverse,
it's a hope-and-a-half:
too much and too little at once.

It's a train that suddenly
stops with no station around,
and we can hear the cricket,
and, leaning out the carriage

door, we vainly contemplate
a wind we feel that stirs
the blooming meadows, the meadows
made imaginary by this stop.

MUSIC

Take me by the hand;
it's so easy for you, Angel,
for you are the road
even while being immobile.

You see, I'm scared no one
here will look for me again;
I couldn't make use of
whatever was given,

so they abandoned me.
At first the solitude
charmed me like a prelude,
but so much music wounded me.

CLOUDS

These laborers of rain, these heavy clouds,
see how evening takes them on celestial vacations;
a delirium of uselessness has gripped them,
and their vacationing edges dare transparencies.

They nonchalantly imitate mountains and islands
and propose luminous caps to the shipwrecks of sight.
And later, in front of the moon,
how many of their profiles will become feminine.

Around them, these depths which soon
ought to hold the numberless worlds, blanch.
And a friend who doesn't watch herself says: Nice,
and closes herself on the unutterable.

THE LIFE OF MARY

TRANSLATED BY J. B. LEISHMAN

THE BIRTH OF MARY

O what it must have cost them, the hosts of Heaven,
not to burst into song, as though into tears,
knowing so well: this night would the mother be given,
be born for the Boy, the One coming before many
     years.

They hovered in silence, a gesture their sole indication
of where the lone farm lay belonging to Joachim.
Ah, they felt in themselves and in space the pure
     concentration,
but not one of them dared to go down to him.

For the pair were distraught enough, there was such a
     to-doing.
A neighbour, a know-all, came and tried to arrange,
and the old man thoughtfully went and hushed the
     mooing
of a dark cow. For things were never so strange.

THE PRESENTATION OF MARY
IN THE TEMPLE

To grasp how she was then, try if you can
to place yourself where pillars mount to ceilings
which are in you; where you can share the feelings
of steps; where arches take great risks to span
the gulf of inward space you could not part with,
since it was made of such huge blocks to start with,
heaving it from you would have meant the fall
of your whole being: if you'd had the strength.
When you are stone-filled, when you've reached
        the length
of being just vault, vista, entrance, wall, –
seize the great curtain hung before your face,
hiding the gleam of objects so exalted
breathing is checked by them, blind groping halted:
try, with both hands, to pull it back, a trace.
High, low, near, far, palaces fill the place;
banisters stream, as stair from stair emerges,
broaden, then balance on such dizzy verges
you're seized with vertigo. Near things efface
their outlines in the cloud of smoke that surges
from burning censers; but each levelled ray
from those far off makes for you, straight and lancing, –
and if clear light from fire-bowls should be dancing
on robes that very slowly come your way:

could it be borne?
She came though, and she raised
her eyes, and stood there taking it all in.
(A child, a little girl between grown women.)
And went up to the pampered splendour then,
(it swayed a little) calmly, quite undazed:
so far was all that had been built by men
inferior to the voice that praised
within her heart. And the desire
to go by inner signs, by these alone.
Her parents thought they lifted her; the one,
so menacing, whose breast flashed jewels' fire,
seemed to receive her: but she went through all,
the child, out of their hands into her fate,
prepared already, higher than the hall,
pressing more hardly than the building's weight.

ANNUNCIATION TO MARY

The angel's entrance (you must realize)
was not what made her frightened. The surprise
he gave her by his coming was no more
than sun- or moon-beam stirring on the floor
would give another, – she had long since grown
used to the form that angels wear, descending;
never imagining this coming-down
was hard for them. (O it's past comprehending,
how pure she was. Did not, one day, a hind
that rested in a wood, watchfully staring,
feel her deep influence, and did it not
conceive the unicorn, then, without pairing,
the pure beast, beast which light begot. –)
No, not to see him enter, but to find
the youthful angel's countenance inclined
so near to her; that when he looked, and she
looked up at him, their looks so merged in one,
the world outside grew vacant suddenly,
and all things being seen, endured and done
were crowded into them: just she and he;
eye and its pasture, vision and its view,
here at this point and at this point alone: –
see, this arouses fear. Such fear both knew.

Then he sang out and made his tidings known.

MARY'S VISITATION

In those first days she moved lightly still,
though she grew aware from time to time
of her marvellous body on a hill, –
and she rested, breathing, from her climb

to the heights of Juda. But her own,
not the fields', abundance lay around her;
walking on she felt: O a profounder
sense of greatness never has been known.

And it moved her, entering, to laying
her hand on the riper body there.
And the women came together swaying
and they touched each other's robes and hair.

Each, big with the shrine that she was keeping,
soothed her cousin and forgot her fear.
Ah the Saviour was a flower still, sleeping,
but the other felt the Baptist leaping
in her womb, for joy, to have him near.

JOSEPH'S SUSPICION

And the angel, striving to explain,
told the man who stood shut-fisted, surly:
Can't you see that she is pure as early
dawn – does not each fold there make it plain?

But the shadow stayed upon his brow.
What, he growled, has changed her? The reply
then came loudly: Joiner, even now
can't you see the hand of the Most High?

You who work with boards, is your pride such
you would argue with the One who urges
buds to fullness, at whose quiet touch,
and from this same wood, the green emerges?

Then at last he saw. And when he lifted
his scared look to meet the angel's gaze,
found him gone. At that the slowly-shifted
heavy cap came off. Then he sang praise.

ANNUNCIATION TO THE SHEPHERDS
FROM ABOVE

Look up, you men. Men at the fire there, you
familiar with the sky's unbounded ways,
star-readers, hither! Look, I am a new
uprising star. My being is one blaze,
so filled with light the firmament is too
small now to hold me and my powerful rays,
for all its depth. Do let my splendour throw
its beams right into you: oh the dark sight,
the gloomy hearts, destinies black as night
that you're brim-full of. Shepherds, I am so
alone in you. Yet, now, there's room for me.
Weren't you astonished: the big bread-fruit-tree
was casting shadow. Well, that shade *I* threw.
O you undaunted, if you only knew
how even now upon each gazing face
the future shines. Much will be taking place
in that clear light. To you I can speak out,
you have discretion; straight souls, free from doubt,
you hear tongues everywhere. Warmth speaks
    and rain,
wind, birds' flight, what you are; no one sound is
more than another, and no vanities
fatten themselves. You don't detain
things in that interval the breast, to be

tormented there. As his own ecstasy
streams through an angel, earthliness can make
its way through you. And should a thornbush take
fire suddenly, the Infinite could still
call to you from it; Cherubim would fill,
if any deigned to walk where your flocks graze,
those hearts of yours with no alarmed surprise:
you'd fall upon your faces and give praise,
and name this earth still and not Paradise.

But all this was. A new thing dawns to-day
for which the round earth seeks to grow more wide.
What is a thornbush now: God feels his way
into a virgin's womb. I am the ray
thrown by her inwardness, which is your guide.

THE BIRTH OF CHRIST

If you lacked simplicity, how then
should this fall to you that midnight skies
are ashine with? God, who stormed at men,
mild in you now comes to mortal eyes.

That he's not more great – does this surprise?

What is greatness? Sweepingly his fate
cuts across all human measurings.
No star, even, has a path so straight.
Look, these coming now are great, these kings

dragging to your lap, as presents, things

which, they hold, are greater far than all.
Maybe they astound you, gifts like these: –
look, though, how within your folded shawl
he excels already all one sees.

Amber, shipped across great distances,

golden ornaments and fragrant spice
such as makes the heavy senses swim:

these were pleasures over in a trice,
and regretted when their power grew dim.

But (as you will see): joy comes of him.

REST ON THE FLIGHT INTO EGYPT

These, who late so breathlessly had flown
from the scene where blood of infants flowed,
oh, to what a greatness they had grown,
imperceptibly, upon the road.

Scarcely had their furtive backward glancing
melted anguish, dissipated dread,
when they brought, on their grey mule advancing,
danger to whole towns that lay ahead;

for when they, in this huge land so small,
neared strong temples where the heathen prayed,
idols there, as if they'd been betrayed,
grew demented, crashed down, one and all.

Who could have supposed that all this mad
rage would greet their coming on the scene?
And they feared themselves, this power they had,
while the babe alone remained serene.

Yet, they had to sit down and recover
for a little, where a tree spread wide.
When – the tree that silently hung over
came, as though to serve them, to their side,

bowing down. That very tree, whose wreath
has until eternity the sleeping
Pharaoh's brow entrusted to its keeping,
stooped. Felt other crown's new green up-leaping.
And they sat, as in a dream, beneath.

OF THE MARRIAGE AT CANA

Could she fail to take pride in this son
who for her turned plainest things to treasure?
When he came, was not high night as one
half deranged, though used to largest measure?

Was there not unheard-of glory later
in that time when he was lost and found:
when earth's wisest, knowing him for greater,
changed their tongues for ears? Did not the sound

of his voice remake the dwelling? Oh,
surely she'd a hundred times denied
outward shining to her joy and pride.
Following, she felt her wonder grow.

But when all those wedding-guests were seated
and they suddenly ran out of wine, –
she could not take in that he had greeted
with refusal her entreating sign.

Then he did it. Just what *she* had done
grew clear afterwards: for now at last
his real wonder-working had begun
and the die for sacrifice was cast

irretrievably. It had been, truly,
fore-ordained. But was it time yet? She:
she had forced the pace of things unduly
in the blindness of her vanity.

She was joyful with the others bidden
to the festive meal; nor understood
that the water of her tears, yet hidden,
turned, as this wine reddened, into blood.

BEFORE THE PASSION

Oh, willing this, you should not have been born
of woman's body: saviours should by right
be quarried from the mountains, brought to light
where out of what is hard the hard is torn.

When you lay waste the valley that you love
does it not grieve you? I am helpless, look;
I only have a milk- and tear-filled brook
and you were always over and above.

You were announced to me with so much splendour.
Why did you not rush wildly from my womb?
If you want tigers tearing you asunder,
why was I brought up in the women's room,

to weave for you a garment soft and clean
where not one trace of joining should be found
harsh to the touch: – thus my whole life has been,
and you have suddenly turned nature round.

PIETÀ

Full is my woe now, speechlessly it all
brims up in me. Rigid am I, as stone
at the stone's core.
Thus hard, I only see one thing:
that you have grown –
... and you have grown
into a grief so large,
it is beyond my heart to grasp
and reaches out.
Now you lie right across my womb,
now I can nevermore
give birth to you.

MARY AT PEACE WITH THE
RISEN LORD

What they experienced then: is it not
beyond all secrets sweet,
and all still terrestrial:
when he, a little pale still from the grave,
disburdened came to her:
in all parts resurrected.
Oh, to her first. How they were both then
inexpressibly healing.
Yes, healing, just that. They did not require
to touch at all strongly.
He laid, for barely a second,
his soon to become
eternal hand on her woman's shoulder.
And they had started,
quietly as trees in the springtime,
immensely together,
this season of their
farthest-reaching communion.

OF THE DEATH OF MARY

I

The same great angel from whose lips she heard,
long since, the Saviour promised to her womb,
waiting her notice, stood there in the room.
'The time has come for you to appear.' His word,
still awful, found still the obedient,
wholly-consenting handmaid. But he, nearing
endlessly, radiant, was disappearing
as if into her countenance – and sent
for the disciples scattered far and wide
to climb once more together that sloped way
to the Last Supper house. All stepped inside
more heavily, and heart-sick: there she lay
on the small bed, who'd so mysteriously
been plunged in sorrow and electedness;
she lay as though unused, all ravageless,
and hearkened to the angels' psalmody.
But seeing now their candles and how they
all waited there, she forced herself to part
from this too-glorious sound, and gave away
both of her dresses, gave with all her heart,
lifting her eyes to each in turn ... (O those
well-springs of tears, what rivers they had shed.)

*　*　*

Then she lay back in weakness on her bed
and drew Jerusalem and Heaven so close,
that, when her spirit came to separate,
it only had to stretch a tiny distance:
already He, who knew its whole existence,
was lifting it to its divine estate.

II

Before she came there, who would have suspected
that abundant Heaven was incomplete?
He had assumed his place, the Resurrected,
but for those four-and-twenty years the seat
next him was empty. And they had begun
to get used to this purest gap, now seeming
all but healed, since full of brightness streaming,
with such marvellous beauty, from the Son.

So she did not, crossing Heaven's threshold,
approach him, though this longing was transcendent;
there was no room, for He was there, resplendent
with radiance it hurt her to behold.
But when, a touching figure, – adding light
to light – she joined the souls newly assembled
and whom she modestly would have resembled,
from ambush in her burst out rays so bright,
the angel caught and blinded by them trembled
and cried out in a loud voice: Who is she?

There was astonishment. Then all could see
how God the Father stooped down and restrained
our Lord, so that a mild half-light remained
and wavered softly round the empty place
which now was as a little grief, a trace
of loneliness, left over from the dearth
and dry affliction he had borne on earth. –
All watched her. As if feeling: I must be
his longest pain, she leant round anxiously
and gazed: – and then rushed forward. But this drew
the angels to her side. With blissful song
they led her to him, helping her along,
and carried her for the last step or two.

III

But when Thomas the Apostle drew
near the sepulchre, belatedly,
forth there came to him the angel, who,
long foreseeing, spoke commandingly:

Push the stone aside. Does your heart wonder
where she is, that was so moved by her?
Look, she was a little while thereunder
buried like a bag of lavender,

that the earth might have such fragrance stealing
from each fold as finest cloths are lent.
All that's dead, decayed, (you can't help feeling)
has been stupefied by her sweet scent.

See the linen shroud, its blinding whiteness:
are there greens where bleaching can be done
half so well? The stainless body's brightness
was more purifying than the sun.

And so gentle was her vanishing
out of it, it scarcely seems forsaken.
But the heavens above are being shaken:
man, kneel down and look at me and sing.

From
SONNETS TO ORPHEUS

TRANSLATED BY J. B. LEISHMAN

A tree ascending there. O pure transcension!
O Orpheus sings! O tall tree in the ear!
All noise suspended, yet in that suspension
what new beginning, beckoning, change, appear!

Creatures of silence pressing through the clear
disintricated wood from lair and nest;
and neither cunning, it grew manifest,
had made them breathe so quietly, nor fear,

but only hearing. Roar, cry, bell they found
within their hearts too small. And where before
less than a hut had harboured what came thronging,

a refuge tunnelled out of dimmest longing
with lowly entrance through a quivering door,
you built them temples in their sense of sound.

And almost maiden-like was what drew near
from that twin-happiness of song and lyre,
and shone so clearly through her spring attire,
and made herself a bed within my ear.

And slept in me sleep that was everything:
the trees I'd always loved, the unrevealed,
treadable distances, the trodden field,
and all my strangest self-discovering.

She slept the world. O singing god, and stayed,
while you were shaping her, with no desire
to wake, and only rose to fall asleep?

Where is her death? Oh, shall you find this deep
unsounded theme before your song expire?
Sinking to where from me? ... Almost a maid ...

A god can do it. But can a man expect
to penetrate the narrow lyre and follow?
His sense is discord. Temples for Apollo
are not found where two heart-ways intersect.

For song, as taught by you, is not desire,
not wooing of something finally attained;
song is existence. For the god unstrained.
But when shall we *exist*? And he require

the earth and heavens to exist for us?
It's more than being in love, boy, though your ringing
voice may have flung your dumb mouth open thus:

learn to forget those fleeting ecstasies.
Far other is the breath of real singing.
An aimless breath. A stirring in the god. A breeze.

Step now and then, you gentle-hearted,
into the breath not breathed for you,
let it blow over your cheeks, and, parted,
quiver behind you, united anew.

Blissful spirits no conflict harrows,
starters, surely, of many a heart.
Bows for arrows and targets for arrows,
divinelier smiling through tears that smart.

Be not afraid of suffering, render
heaviness back to the earth again;
mountains are heavy, and seas, and the tender

trees that in childhood you set in their places
have grown too heavy for you to sustain.
Ah, but the breezes ... ah, but the spaces ...

Raise no commemorating stone. The roses
shall blossom every summer for his sake.
For this is Orpheus. His metamorphosis
in this one and in that. We should not take

thought about other names. Once and for all,
it's Orpheus when there's song. He comes and goes.
Is it not much if sometimes, by some small
number of days, he shall outlive the rose?

Could you but feel his passing's needfulness!
Though he himself may dread the hour drawing
        nigher.
Already, when his words pass earthliness,

he passes with them far beyond your gaze.
His hands unhindered by the trellised lyre,
in all his over-steppings he obeys.

Does he belong here? No, his spreading
nature from either domain has sprung.
Withes would they weave in a cunninger wedding,
hands to which roots of the willow had clung.

Going to bed, never leave on the table
bread or milk, forcing the dead to rise. –
He shall invoke them, he who is able
to mingle in mildness of closing eyes

their appearance with all that we view;
he for whom magic of earth-smoke and rue
shall be clear as the clearest link between things.

Nothing can weaken the image he saves,
whether from dwellings, whether from graves,
glorifying pitchers or bracelets or rings.

Praising, that's it! As a praiser and blesser
he came like the ore from the taciturn mine.
Came with his heart, oh, transient presser,
for men, of a never-exhaustible wine.

Voice never fails him for things lacking lustre,
sacred example will open his mouth.
All becomes vineyard, all becomes cluster,
warmed by his sympathy's ripening south.

Crypts and the mouldering kings who lie there
do not belie his praising, neither
doubt, when a shadow obscures our days.

He is a messenger always attendant,
reaching far through their gates resplendent
dishes of fruit for the dead to praise.

Only by him with whose lays
shades were enraptured
may the celestial praise
faintly be captured.

Only who tasted their own
flower with the sleeping
holds the most fugitive tone
ever in keeping.

Make but the mirroring pond
's fleetingly tendered
image endure!

Not till both here and beyond
voices are rendered
lasting and pure.

Hail, the spirit able to unite!
For we truly live our lives in symbol,
and with tiny paces move our nimble
clocks beside our real day and night.

Still we somehow act in true relation,
we that find ourselves we know not where.
Distant station feels for distant station –
what seemed empty space could bear . . .

purest tension. Harmony of forces!
Do not just our limited resources
keep all interference from your flow?

Does the farmer, anxiously arranging,
ever reach to where the seed is changing
into summer? Does not Earth bestow?

Banana, rounded apple, russet pear,
gooseberry . . . Does not all this convey
life and death into your mouth? . . . It's there! . . .
Read it on a child's face any day,

when it tastes them. What infinity!
Can't you feel inside your mouth a growing
mysteriousness, and, where words were, a flowing
of suddenly released discovery?

Dare to say what 'apple' has implied!
Sweetness, concentrated, self-repressing,
slowly yielding to the tongue's caressing,

growing awake, transparent, clarified,
double-meaning'd, sunshine-full, terrestrial: –
O experience, feeling, joy, – celestial!

Our life-long neighbours, flower, vine-leaf, fruit,
they do not merely speak the season's speech.
These things so brightly manifest, that reach
from darkness, gleam, it may be, with the mute

envy of those through whom the earth grows strong.
What do we know about the part they play?
To mix their unused marrow with the clay
has been their second-nature for so long.

But do they do it of their own accords?
Is it by sullen slaves that these clenched fruits
are laboured and thrust forth to us, their lords?

Are *they* the lords, who sleep beside the roots,
and grant us, what their plenty never misses,
this middle-thing, made of dumb strength and kisses?

Undermost he, the earth-bound
root of uprearing
multitudes, source underground,
never appearing.

Helmet and hunting-horn,
words of the ageing,
rage between brothers-born,
women assuaging.

Branch on branch, time on time,
vainly they spire . . .
One free! Oh, climb . . . oh, climb . . .

One, though the others drop,
curves, as it scales the top,
into a lyre.

Master, there's something new
droning and drumming.
It has its heralds too,
praising its coming.

Ill though our ears withstand
such perturbation,
now the machines demand
their celebration.

Source of our weakness
now, and in vengeful rage
ruining our heritage,

us shall these things at length,
us, who supply their strength,
serve in all meekness.

Change though the world may as fast
as cloud-collections,
home to the changeless at last
fall all perfections.

Over the thrust and the throng,
freer and higher,
echoes your preluding song,
god with the lyre.

Sorrow we misunderstand,
love we have still to begin,
death and what's hidden therein

await unveiling.
Song alone circles the land,
hallowing and hailing.

But what shall I offer you, Master, say,
you who taught all creatures to hear? –
The remembered evening of one spring day,
in Russia: a horse drawing near ...

White, coming up from the village alone,
on one fetlock a tethering-block,
to spend the night alone, on his own:
how gaily he tossed the shock

of his mane in time to his mounting mood
on that rudely encumbered race!
How they leapt, the springs of the equine blood!

He had followed the call of space.
He sang and he listened – your cycle swept
unbrokenly through him.
                    His image: accept.

We wax for waning.
Count, though, Time's journeying
as but a little thing
in the Remaining.

End of unmeasured
hasting will soon begin;
only what's leisured
leads us within.

Boys, don't be drawn too far
into attempts at flight,
into mere swiftness. – Look

how rested all things are:
shadow and fall of light,
blossom and book.

Breathing, invisible poem! That great
world-space, at each inhalation
exchanged for this human existence.
      Counter-weight
of my rhythmical realization.

Single wavelet, whose slowly
gathering sea am I;
you, of all possible seas most frugal and lowly, –
space laid-by.

Of all these places in space, how many a one
has been within me already. Many a wind
seems like a son.

Do you know me, air, still full of my
      dwelling-places?
You, the one-time smooth-skinned
rondure and leaf of my phrases.

Mirrors: no one has yet distilled with
patient knowledge your fugitive
essence. You spaces in time, that are filled with
holes like those of a sieve.

Squandering the empty ball-room's pomp,
deep as forests when twilight broods . . .
And, like sixteen-pointers, the lustres romp
through your virginal solitudes.

Pictures crowd you at times. A few
seem to be taken right within you,
shyly to others you wave adieu.

There, though, the fairest will always be,
till through to her lips withheld continue
Narcissus, released into lucency.

Flowers, whose kinship with ordering hands
        we are able
to feel at last (girls' hands, of once, of to-day),
who often, strewn all over the garden table,
tired and tenderly injured, lay

waiting for water to come, once more repealing
death already begun, – and now
uplifted again between the poles of those feeling,
magnetical fingers you have to allow

can be far kinder than delicate you had guessed
on coming round in the jug, to find
you were cooling and slowly exhaling the warmth
        of girls, like things confessed,

like tiring sins remembered in drowsy gloom,
despoiling of you committed, to bind
you to them once more, who blend with you
        in their bloom.

You few, the one-time sharers of childhood's treasure
in the city's scattered garden walks,
how we met and awoke in each other a hesitant
        pleasure,
and, like the lamb with the scroll that talks,

spoke without speaking. If sometimes happiness
        found us,
no one possessed it. Whose could it be?
And how it would melt among all those moving
        around us,
and the long year's anxiety.

Unconcerning carriages rolling and swerving,
houses surrounding us strongly – untruthfully,
        though, and never
a thing that knew us. Was anything real at all?

Nothing. Only the balls. Their glorious curving.
No, not even the children ... Though one would ever
pass, ah, fleetingly! under the falling ball.

Anticipate all farewells, as were they behind you
now, like the winter going past.
For through some winter you feel such wintriness
        bind you,
your then out-wintering heart will always outlast.

Dead evermore in Eurydice, mount with more singing,
mount to relation more pure with more celebrant,
        tongue.
Here, in this realm of the dwindlers and dregs,
        be a ringing
glass, which has, even though shivered to pieces,
        been rung.

Be – and, perceiving in that which is being's negation
merely the infinite ground of your fervent vibration,
beat, through this never-again, to the fullest amount.

To the stock of used-up, as well as of dumb and
        decaying
things within copious Nature, those sums beyond
        saying,
count yourself joyfully in and destroy the account.

O fountain mouth, you mouth that can respond
so inexhaustibly to all who ask
with one, pure, single saying. Marble mask
before the water's flowing face. Beyond,

the aqueducts' long derivation. Past
the tombs, from where the Apennines begin,
they bring your saying to you, which at last,
over the grizzled age of your dark chin,

falls to the waiting basin, crystal-clear;
falls to the slumbering recumbent ear,
the marble ear, with which you still confer.

One of earth's ears. With her own lonely mood
she thus converses. Let a jug intrude,
she'll only think you've interrupted her.

Still the god remains an ever-growing
wholeness we have irritably burst.
We are sharp, for we insist on knowing,
he exists serenely and dispersed.

Even gifts of purest consecration
only find acceptance in so much
as he turns in moveless contemplation
to the end we do not touch.

Only those who dwell
out of sight can taste the spring we hear,
when the god has silently assented.

With its brawling we must be contented.
And the lamb's more silent instinct's clear
when it begs us for its bell.

Where, in what ever-blissfully watered gardens, upon
        what trees,
out of, oh, what gently dispetalled flower-cups do these
so strange-looking fruits of consolation mature?
Delicious, when, now and then, you pick one up in the
        poor

trampled field of your poverty. Time and again you
        find
yourself lost in wonder over the size of the fruit,
over its wholesomeness, over its smooth, soft rind,
and that neither the heedless bird above nor jealous
        worm at the root

has been before you. Are there, then, trees where
        angels will congregate,
trees invisible leisurely gardeners so curiously
        cultivate,
that, without being ours, they bear for us fruits like
        those?

Have we, then, never been able, we shadows and
        shades,
with our doing that ripens too early and then as
        suddenly fades,
to disturb that even-tempered summer's repose?

Dancer: you transmutation
of all going-by into going: what you have wrought!
And your finishing whirl, that tree of mere animation,
how it took over the year you had flyingly caught!

Did not its crown, that your swaying might settle to
      swarming,
suddenly blossom with stillness? Above that, too,
was there not sunnily, was there not summerly
      warming
all the warmth that exhaled from you?

Nay, it was able, your tree of rapture, to bear.
Are they not, all its fruits that so peacefully shine,
jug streaked with ripeness, vase further ripened, still
      there?

And does not your mark in their paintings still meet
      the discerning –
that of your eyebrows' darker line
swiftly inscribed on the wall of your own swift
      turning?

Gold dwells somewhere at ease in the pampering bank,
mixing with thousands on intimate terms. But to any
coin that blind man begging, to even a penny,
seems but a desolate place, a chink in a dusty plank.

Money shines out from the shops in its own dimension,
plausibly masking in silk, carnation, and fur.
He, though, silently stands in the breath-suspension
of all the money breathing, asleep or astir.

Oh, how does it ever close at night, that perpetually
    open hand?
Fate to-morrow will fetch it back and display it,
bright, poor, endlessly fragile, year after year.

Could but at last some gazer, astoundedly coming to
    understand,
celebrate its persistence! – Only a singer could say it.
Only a god could hear.

Sing those gardens, my heart, poured as into a glass,
gardens you have not known, transparent, untrampled.
Waters and roses of Ispahan or Shiras,
blissfully sing them, praise them, the unexampled.

Show that by you, my heart, they are never missed:
pleasure for you their ripening figs are preparing,
you with their breezes, almost visibly bearing
fragrance of blossoming branches, can always tryst.

Know that no want exists for, no hand bereaving
takes from, the acted resolution: to *be*.
Silken thread, you have entered into the weaving.

Feel, with what pattern soever you're inwardly blended
(even a scene from the story of Agony),
feel that the whole, the praisable, carpet's intended.

Call me to your lonely meeting-places
with the hour that always says you nay:
suppliantly near you, like dogs' faces,
time and time again, though, turned away,

when at last you think it is yours.
Things thus snatched from you are most your own.
We are free – dismissed from those same doors
where we thought such welcome had been shown.

Anxiously we hanker for a holdfast,
we, too youthful sometimes for the old past,
and too old for what has never been.

We, whose righteousness depends how far we
praise, for branch and axe and sweetness are we
of a peril ripening unseen.

Oh, delight leaping up ever-new when we loosen
    the soil!
Hardly a hand lent the earliest darers assistance.
Towns arose none the less on gulfs to a blessed
    existence,
pitchers were filled none the less with water and oil.

Gods, – we plan them in bold provisional sketches
cross-grained Fate takes from us and flings to the past.
Still, they *are* the Immortals. Our spirit outstretches,
hearkening-out the one that will hear it at last.

We, but one race for millennia, growing ever greater,
age after age, with that child of the future whose birth
shall so entirely surpass and astonish us, later.

We, so immeasurably ventured, what aeons attend us!
And only taciturn Death knows what we are worth,
and how much it always pays him to lend us.

Hark, the earliest harrows striving
already; the rhythm of man once more
breaks the tense stillness around reviving
pre-vernal earth. What has come before

seems to return as unstaled as ever.
No new-comer, it comes like new.
Looked for again and again, you never
could capture it. Always it captured you.

Sunset splashes the wintered oaken
leaves with a brown that is yet to be.
Sometimes breezes exchange a token.

Black are the hedges. But heaps of dung
crouch more satedly black on the lea.
Hours grow more eternally young.

How it thrills us, the bird's clear cry . . .
Any cry that was always there.
Children, playing in the open air,
children already go crying by

real cries. Cry chance in. Through crevasses
in that same space whereinto, as dreaming
men into dreams, the pure bird-cry passes
they drive their splintering wedge of screaming.

Where are we? Freer and freer, we gyre
only half up, kites breaking
loose, with our frills of laughter flaking

away in the wind. – Make the criers a choir,
singing god! that resurgently waking
may bear on its waters the head and the lyre.

Does it exist, though, Time the destroyer?
When will it scatter the tower on the resting hill?
This heart, the eternal gods' eternal enjoyer,
when shall the Demiurge ravish and spill?

Are we really such tremblingly breakable
things as Destiny tries to pretend?
Does childhood's promise, deep, unmistakable,
down in the roots, then, later, end?

Ah, Mutability's spectre!
out through the simple accepter
you, like a vapour, recede.

We, though we wax but for waning,
fill none the less for remaining
powers a celestial need.

Oh, come and go, you almost child, enhancing
for one brief hour the figure of the dance
to part of that pure constellated dancing
where, subject as we are to change and chance,

we beat dull nature. For she only started
hearing with all her ears at Orpheus' song.
And you still moved with motion then imparted,
and shrank a little if a tree seemed long

in treading with you the remembered pace.
You knew it still, that passage where the lyre
soundingly rose, the unimagined centre,

and practised all your steps in hope to enter
that theme again, whirling to one entire
communion with your friend both feet and face.

Silent friend of those far from us, feeling
how your breath is still enlarging space,
fill the sombre belfry with your pealing.
What consumes you now is growing apace

stronger than the feeding strength it borrows.
Be, as Change will have you, shade or shine.
Which has grieved you most of all your sorrows?
Turn, if drinking's bitter, into wine.

Be, in this immeasurable night,
at your senses' cross-ways magic cunning,
be the sense of their mysterious tryst.

And, should earthliness forget you quite,
murmur to the quiet earth: I'm running.
Tell the running water: I exist.

THE DUINO ELEGIES

TRANSLATED BY J. B. LEISHMAN
AND STEPHEN SPENDER

THE FIRST ELEGY

Who, if I cried, would hear me among the angelic
orders? And even if one of them suddenly
pressed me against his heart, I should fade in the
        strength of his
stronger existence. For Beauty's nothing
but beginning of Terror we're still just able to bear,
and why we adore it so is because it serenely
disdains to destroy us. Every angel is terrible.
And so I repress myself, and swallow the call-note
of depth-dark sobbing. Alas, who is there
we can make use of? Not angels, not men;
and even the noticing beasts are aware
that we don't feel very securely at home
in this interpreted world. There remains, perhaps,
some tree on a slope, to be looked at day after day,
there remains for us yesterday's walk and the long-drawn
        loyalty
of a habit that liked us and stayed and never gave notice.
Oh, and there's Night, there's Night, when wind full of
        cosmic space
feeds on our faces: for whom would she not remain,
longed for, mild disenchantress, painfully there
for the lonely heart to achieve? Is she lighter for lovers?
Alas, with each other they only conceal their lot!
Don't you know *yet*? – Fling the emptiness out of your arms

165

to broaden the spaces we breathe – maybe that the birds
will feel the extended air in more fervent flight.
Yes, the Springs had need of you. Many a star
was waiting for you to perceive it. Many a wave
would rise in the past towards you; or else, perhaps,
as you went by an open window, a violin
would be utterly giving itself. All this was commission.
But were you equal to it? Were you not still
distraught by expectancy, as though all were announcing
some beloved's approach? (As if you could hope
to house her, with all those great strange thoughts
going in and out and often staying overnight!)
Should you be longing, though, sing the great lovers:
    the fame
of all they can feel is far from immortal enough.
Those – you envied them almost, those forsaken,
    you found
so far beyond the requited in loving. Begin
ever anew their never-attainable praise.
Consider: the Hero continues, even his setting
was a pretext for further existence, an ultimate birth.
But lovers are taken back by exhausted Nature
into herself, as though such creative force
could not be exerted twice. Does Gaspara Stampa
mean enough to you yet, and that any girl,
    whose beloved
has slipped away, might feel, from that far intenser

example of loving: 'Could I but become like her!'?
Should not these oldest sufferings be finally growing
fruitfuller for us? Is it not time that, in loving,
we freed ourselves from the loved one, and, quivering,
    endured:
as the arrow endures the string, to become,
    in the gathering out-leap,
something more than itself? For staying is nowhere.
Voices, voices. Hearken, my heart, as only
saints once hearkened: so, that, the giant call
lifted them off the ground; they, though, impossibles,
went on kneeling and paid no heed,
such was their hearkening. Not that you could bear God's
voice, by a long way. But hark to the suspiration,
the uninterrupted news that grows out of silence.
Rustling towards you now from those youthfully-dead.
Whenever you entered a church in Rome or in Naples
were you not always being quietly addressed by
    their fate?
Or else an inscription sublimely imposed itself on you,
as, lately, the tablet in Santa Maria Formosa.
What they require of me? that I should gently remove
the appearance of suffered injustice, that hinders
a little, at times, their purely-proceeding spirits.

True, it is strange to inhabit the earth no longer,
to use no longer customs scarcely acquired,

not to interpret roses, and other things
that promise so much, in terms of a human future;
to be no longer all that one used to be
in endlessly anxious hands, and to lay aside
even one's proper name like a broken toy.
Strange, not to go on wishing one's wishes. Strange,
to see all that was once relation so loosely fluttering
hither and thither in space. And it's hard, being dead,
and full of retrieving before one begins to perceive
a little eternity. – All of the living, though,
make the mistake of drawing too sharp distinctions.
Angels (it's said) would be often unable to tell
whether they moved among living or dead. The eternal
torrent whirls all the ages through either realm
for ever, and sounds above their voices in both.

They've finally no more need of us, the early-departed,
one's gently weaned from terrestrial things as one mildly
outgrows the breasts of a mother. But we,
    that have need of
such mighty secrets, we, for whom sorrow's so often
source of blessedest progress, could we exist
    without them?
Is the story in vain, how once, in the mourning
    for Linos,
venturing earliest music pierced barren numbness,
    and how,

in the startled space an almost deified youth
suddenly quitted for ever, emptiness first
felt the vibration that now lifts us and comforts
and helps?

THE SECOND ELEGY

Every Angel is terrible. Still, though, alas!
I invoke you, almost deadly birds of the soul,
knowing about you. Where are the days of Tobias,
when one of the shining-most stood on the simple
     threshold,
a little disguised for the journey, no longer appalling,
(a youth to the youth as he curiously peered outside).
Let the archangel perilous now, from behind the stars,
step but a step down hitherwards: high up-beating,
our heart would out-beat us. Who are you?

Early successes, favourites of fond Creation,
ranges, summits, dawn-red ridges
of all forthbringing, – pollen of blossoming godhead,
junctures of light, corridors, stairways, thrones,
chambers of essence, shields of felicity, tumults
of stormily-rapturous feeling, and suddenly, separate,
mirrors, drawing up again their own
outstreamed beauty into their own faces.

For we, when we feel, evaporate; oh, we
breathe ourselves out and away; from ember to ember
yielding a fainter scent. True, someone may tell us:
'You've got in my blood, the room, the Spring's

growing full of you' ... What's the use? He cannot
     retain us,
we vanish within and around him. And those
     that have beauty,
oh, who shall hold them back? Appearance of something
keeps getting up in their faces and going away. Like dew
from the morning grass what's ours exhales from us,
     like the heat
from a smoking dish. O smile, whither? O upward gaze:
new, warm, vanishing wave of the heart – alas,
but we *are* all that. Does the cosmic space
we dissolve into taste of us, then? Do the angels really
only catch up what is theirs, what has streamed
     from them, or at times,
as though through an oversight, is a little of our
essence in it as well? Is there just so much of us
mixed with their features as that vague look
     in the faces
of pregnant women? Unmarked by them in the whirl
     of their
coming back to themselves. (How should they remark it?)

Lovers, indeed, if only they could, might utter
strange things in the midnight air. For it seems that
     everything's

trying to hide us. Look, the trees exist; the houses
we live in still stand where they were. We only
pass everything by like a transposition of air.
And all combines to suppress us, partly, perhaps,
as shame, and partly as inexpressible hope.

Lovers, to you, each satisfied in the other,
I turn with my question about us. You grasp
        yourselves. Have you proofs?
Look, with me it may happen at times that my hands
grow aware of each other, or else that my
        hard-worn face
seeks refuge within them. That gives me a little
sensation. But who, just for that, could presume
        to exist?
You, though, that go on growing
in the other's rapture till, overwhelmed, he implores
'No more'; you that under each other's hands
grow more abundant like vintage years;
swooning at times, just because the other
has so expanded: I ask you about us. I know
why you so blissfully touch: because the caress
        you withhold,
because it does not vanish, the place that you
so tenderly cover; because you perceive thereunder
pure duration. Until your embraces almost
promise eternity. Yet, when you've once withstood

the startled first encounter, the window-longing,
and that first walk, just once, through the garden
      together:
Lovers, are you the same? When you lift yourselves
up to each other's lips – drink unto drink:
oh, how strangely the drinker eludes his part!

On Attic stelæ, did not the circumspection
of human gesture amaze you? Were not love and
      farewell
so lightly laid upon shoulders, they seemed to be made
of other stuff than with us? Oh, think of the hands,
how they rest without pressure, though power is there
      in the torsos.
The wisdom of those self-masters was this: hitherto
      it's us;
ours is to touch one another like this; the gods
may press more strongly upon us. But that is the gods'
      affair.
If only we too could discover some pure, contained
narrow, human, own little strip of corn-land
in between river and rock! For our own heart still
      transcends us
even as theirs did. And we can no longer gaze
after it now into pacifying image, or godlike
body, wherein it achieves a grander restraint.

THE THIRD ELEGY

One thing to sing the beloved, another, alas!
that hidden guilty river-god of the blood.
Him she discerns from afar, her lover, what does
    he know
of that Lord of Pleasure, who often, out of his
    lonely heart,
before she'd soothed him, often as though she
    didn't exist,
streaming from, oh, what unknowable depths,
    would uplift
his god-head, uprousing the night to infinite uproar?
Oh, the Neptune within our blood, oh, his terrible
    trident!
Oh, the gloomy blast of his breast from the twisted
    shell!
Hark, how the night grows fluted and hollowed.
    You stars,
is it not from you that the lover's delight in the
    loved one's
face arises? Does not his intimate insight
into her purest face come from the purest star?

It wasn't you, alas! it wasn't his mother
that bent his brows into such an expectant arch.
Not to meet yours, girl feeling him, not to meet yours

did his lips begin to assume that more fruitful curve.
Do you really suppose your gentle approach could have so
convulsed him, you, that wander like wind at dawn?
You terrified his heart, indeed; but more ancient
        terrors
rushed into him in that instant of shattering touch.
Call him ... you can't quite call him away from sombre
        consorting.
He certainly wants to, he does escape; disburdenedly
        settles
into your intimate heart, takes up and begins himself
        there.
Did he ever begin himself, though?
Mother, you made him small, it was you that began
        him;
for you he was new, you arched over those new eyes
the friendly world, averting the one that was strange.
Where, oh, where, are the years when you barred the way
for him, with your slender form, to the surging abyss?
You hid so much from him then; made the nightly-
        suspected room
harmless, and out of your heart full of refuge
mingled more human space with that night-space of his.
Not in the darkness, no, but within your far nearer
        presence
you placed the light, and it shone as though out of
        friendship.

Nowhere a creak you could not explain with a smile,
as though you had long known *when* the floor would
	behave itself thus ...
And he listened to you and was soothed. So much it
	availed,
gently, your rising: his tall cloaked destiny stepped
behind the wardrobe then, and his restless future
that easily got out of place, conformed to the folds
	of the curtain.

And he himself as he lay there in such relief,
dissolving, under his drowsy eyelids, the sweetness
of your light shaping into the sleep he had tasted,
seemed to be under protection ... *Within*, though: who
	could avert,
divert, the floods of origin flowing within him?
Alas! there *was* no caution within that sleeper; sleeping,
yes, but dreaming, yes, but feverish: what he embarked on!
He, so new, so timorous, how he got tangled
in ever-encroaching creepers of inner event,
twisted to primitive patterns, to throttling growths,
	to bestial
preying forms! How he gave himself up to it! Loved.
Loved his interior world, his interior jungle,
that primal forest within, on whose mute
	overthrownness,
light-green, his heart stood. Loved. Left it, continued

out through his own roots into violent beginning
where his tiny birth was already outlived. Descended,
lovingly, into the older blood, the ravines
where Frightfulness lurked, still gorged with his fathers.
        And every
terror knew him, winked, was as though it were waiting.
Yes, Horror smiled at him ... Seldom
did you, Mother, smile so tenderly. How could he help
loving what smiled at him? Long before you
he loved it, for even while you bore him
it was there, dissolved in the water that lightens the seed.

Look, we don't love like flowers, with only a single
season behind us; immemorial sap
mounts in our arms when we love. Oh, maid,
this: that we've loved, *within* us, not one, still to come,
        but all
the innumerable fermentation; not just a single child,
but the fathers, resting like mountain-ruins
within our depths; – but the dry river-bed
of former mothers; – yes, and the whole of that
soundless landscape under its cloudy or
cloudless destiny: – *this* got the start of you, maid.
And you yourself, how can you tell, – you have
        conjured up
prehistoric time in your lover. What feelings
whelmed up from beings gone by! What women

hated you in him! What sinister men
you roused in his youthful veins! Dead children
were trying to reach you . . . Oh, gently, gently
show him daily an honest, confident task done, – guide
     him
close to the garden, give him preponderance
over those nights . . . . . .

                    Withhold him . . . . . .

THE FOURTH ELEGY

O trees of life, what are your signs of winter?
We're not at one. We've no instinctive knowledge,
like migratory birds. Outstript and late,
we force ourselves on winds and find no welcome
from ponds where we alight. We comprehend
flowering and fading simultaneously.
And somewhere lions still roam, all unaware,
while yet their splendour lasts, of any weakness.

We, though, when most intent upon one thing,
can feel the other's dazzlingness. Hostility's
our readiest response. Aren't lovers always
coming to precipices in each other, –
lovers, that looked for spaces, hunting, home?
Then, for the sudden sketchwork of a moment,
a ground of contrast's painfully prepared,
to make us see it. For they're very clear
with us, we that don't know our feeling's shape,
but only that which forms it from outside.
Who's not sat tense before his own heart's curtain?
Up it would go: the scenery was Parting.
Easy to understand. The well-known garden,
swaying a little. Then appeared the dancer.
Not *him*! Enough! However light he foots it,
he's just disguised, and turns into a bourgeois,

and passes through the kitchen to his dwelling.
I will not have these half-filled masks! No, no,
rather the doll. That's full. I'll force myself
to bear the husk, the wire, and even that face
of sheer appearance. Here! I'm in my seat.
Even if the lights go out, even if I'm told
'There's nothing more', – even if greyish draughts
of emptiness come drifting from the stage, –
even if of all my silent forebears none
sits by me any longer, not a woman,
not even the boy with the brown squinting eyes:
I'll still remain. For one can always watch.

Am I not right? You, to whom life would taste
so bitter, Father, when you tasted mine,
that turbid first infusion of my Must,
you kept on tasting as I kept on growing,
and, still arrested by the after-taste
of such queer future, tried my clouded gaze, –
you, who so often, since you died, my Father,
have been afraid within my inmost hope,
surrendering realms of that serenity
the dead are lords of for my bit of fate, –
am I not right? And you, am I not right, –
you that would love me for that small beginning
of love for you I always turned away from,
because the space within your faces changed,

even while I loved it, into cosmic space
where you no longer were..., when I feel like it,
to wait before the puppet stage, – no, rather
gaze so intensely on it that at last
a counterpoising angel has to come
and play a part there, snatching up the husks?
Angel and doll! Then there's at last a play.
Then there unites what we continually
part by our mere existence. Then at last
emerges from our seasons here the cycle
of the whole process. Over and above us,
then, there's the angel playing. Look, the dying, –
surely they must suspect how full of pretext
is all that we accomplish here, where nothing
is what it really is. O hours of childhood,
hours when behind the figures there was more
than the mere past, and when what lay before us
was not the future! True, we were growing,
    and sometimes
made haste to be grown up, half for the sake
of those who'd nothing left but their grown-upness.
Yet, when alone, we entertained ourselves
with everlastingness: there we would stand,
within the gap left between world and toy,
upon a spot which, from the first beginning,
had been established for a pure event.

* * *

Who'll show a child as it is? Who'll place it
within its constellation, with the measure
of distance in its hand? Who'll make its death
from grey bread, that grows hard, – or leave it there,
within the round mouth, like the seeded core
of a nice apple? . . . Minds of murderers
can easily be fathomed. This, though: death,
the whole of death, before life's start, to hold it
so gently and so free from all resentment,
transcends description.

THE FIFTH ELEGY
DEDICATED TO FRAU HERTHA KOENIG

But tell me, who *are* they, these travellers, even a little
more fleeting than we ourselves, – so urgently,
    ever since childhood,
wrung by an (oh, for the sake of whom?)
never-contented will? That keeps on wringing them,
bending them, slinging them, swinging them,
throwing them and catching them back: as though
    from an oily,
smoother air, they come down on the threadbare
carpet, thinned by their everlasting
upspringing, this carpet forlornly
lost in the cosmos.
Laid on like a plaster, as though the suburban sky
had injured the earth there.

                      And hardly there,
upright, shown us: the great initial
letter of Thereness, – than even the strongest
men are rolled once more, in sport, by the ever-
returning grasp, as once by Augustus the Strong
a tin platter at table.

Alas, and round this
centre the rose of onlooking
blooms and unblossoms. Round this

183

pestle, this pistil, caught by its own
dust-pollen, and fertilized over again
to a sham-fruit of boredom, their own
never-realized, so thin-surfacedly gleaming,
lightly sham-smiling boredom.

There, the withered wrinkled lifter,
old now and only drumming,
shrivelled up in his massive hide as though it had
     once contained
two men, and one were already
lying in the churchyard, and this one here had
     survived him,
deaf and sometimes a little
lost in his widowed skin.

And the youngster, the man, like the son of a neck
and a nun: so tautly and smartly filled
with muscle and simpleness.

O you,
a pain that was still quite small
received as a plaything once in one of its
long convalescences. . . .

You, that fall with the thud
only fruits know, unripe,

daily a hundred times from the tree
of mutually built up motion (the tree that,
        swifter than water,
has spring and summer and autumn in
        so many minutes),
fall and rebound on the grave:
sometimes, in half-pauses, a tenderness tries
to steal out over your face to your seldomly
tender mother, but scatters over your body,
whose surface quickly absorbs the timidly rippling,
hardly attempted look ... And again
that man is clapping his hands for the downward
        spring, and before
a single pain has got within range of your ever-
galloping heart, comes the tingling
in the soles of your feet, ahead of the spring that
        it springs from,
chasing into your eyes a few physical tears.
And still, all instinctive,
that smile....

Angel! oh, take it, pluck it, that small-flowered
        herb of healing!
Get a vase to preserve it. Set it among those joys
not yet open to us: in a graceful urn
praise it, with florally soaring inscription:
                                    'Subrisio Saltat.'

Then you, my darling,
mutely elided
by all the most exquisite joys. Perhaps
your frills are happy on your behalf, –
or over your tight young breasts
the green metallic silk
feels itself endlessly spoilt and in need of nothing.
You,
time after time, upon all of the quivering scale-pans
    of balance
freshly laid fruit of serenity,
publicly shown among shoulders.

Where, oh, where in the world is that place in my heart
where they still were far from being *able*, still fell away
from each other like mounting animals, not yet
ready for pairing; –
where weights are still heavy,
and hoops still stagger
away from their vainly
twirling sticks? . . . . .

And then, in this wearisome nowhere, all of a sudden,
the ineffable spot where the pure too-little
incomprehensibly changes, veering
into that empty too-much?
Where the many-digited sum
solves into zero?

Squares, O square in Paris, infinite show-place,
where the modiste Madame Lamort
winds and binds the restless ways of the world,
those endless ribbons, to ever-new
creations of bow, frill, flower, cockade and fruit,
all falsely coloured, to deck
the cheap winter-hats of Fate.

. . . .

Angel: suppose there's a place we know nothing about,
        and there,
on some indescribable carpet, lovers showed all that here
they're for ever unable to manage – their daring
lofty figures of heart-flight,
their towers of pleasure, their ladders,
long since, where ground never was, just quiveringly
propped by each other, – were able to manage it there,
before the ringed onlookers there, countless unmurmuring
        dead:
would not those then fling their last, their for ever
        reserved,
ever-concealed, unknown to us, ever-valid
coins of happiness down before the at last
truthfully smiling pair on the quietened
carpet?

THE SIXTH ELEGY

Fig tree, how long it's been full meaning for me,
the way you almost entirely omit to flower
and into the early-resolute fruit
uncelebratedly thrust your purest secret.
Like the tube of a fountain, your bent bough drives the sap
downwards and up; and it leaps from its sleep, scarce
     waking,
into the joy of its sweetest achievement. Look,
like Jupiter into the swan.

                    . . . . . We, though, we linger,
alas, we glory in flowering; already revealed
we reach the retarded core of our ultimate fruit.
In few the pressure of action rises so strongly
that already they're stationed and glowing in fullness
     of heart,
when, seductive as evening air, the temptation
     to flower,
touching the youth of their mouths, touching their
     eyelids, appears:
only in heroes, perhaps, and those marked for
     early removal,
those in whom gardening Death's differently
     twisted the veins.

These go plunging ahead: preceding their own
victorious smile, as the team of horse in the mildly-
moulded reliefs of Karnak the conquering King.

Yes, the Hero's strangely akin to the youthfully dead.
      Duration
doesn't concern him. His rising's existence.
      Time and again
he takes himself off and enters the changed
      constellation
his changeless peril's assumed. There few could
      find him. But Fate,
grim concealer of us, enraptured all of a sudden,
sings him into the storm of her surging world.
None do I hear like him. There suddenly rushes
      through me,
borne by the streaming air, his dark-echoing tone.

And then how gladly I'd hide from the longing:
      Oh would,
would that I were a boy, and might come to it yet,
      and be sitting,
propped upon arms still to be, and reading of Samson,
how his mother at first bore nothing, and, afterwards, all.

Was he not hero already in you, O mother, and had not
even in you his lordly choosing begun?

Thousands were brewing in the womb and trying
    to be *him,*
but, look! he seized and discarded, chose and
    was able to do.
And if ever he shattered columns, that was the time, when he burst
out of the world of your body into the narrower world,
where he went on choosing and doing. O mothers
    of heroes!
Sources of ravaging rivers! Gorges wherein,
from high on the heart's edge, weeping,
maids have already plunged, victims-to-be for the son.
For whenever the Hero stormed through the halts of love,
each heart beating for him could only lift him beyond it:
turning away, he'd stand at the end of the smiles, another.

THE SEVENTH ELEGY

Not wooing, no longer shall wooing, voice that's
    outgrown it,
be now the form of your cry; though you cried as
    pure as the bird
when the surging season uplifts him, almost forgetting
he's merely a fretful creature and not just a single heart
it's tossing to brightness, to intimate azure. No less
than he, you, too, would be wooing some silent
    companion
to feel you, as yet unseen, some mate in whom a reply
was slowly awaking and warming itself as she listened, –
your own emboldened feeling's enfired fellow-feeling.
Oh, and Spring would understand – not a nook would fail
to re-echo annunciation. Re-echoing first the tiny
questioning pipe a purely affirmative day
quietly invests all round with magnifying stillness.
Then the long flight of steps, the call-steps, up to the
    dreamt-of
temple of what's to come; – then the trill, that fountain
grasped, as it rises, by Falling, in promiseful play,
for another thrusting jet . . . And before it, the Summer!
Not only all those summer dawns, not only
the way they turn into day and stream with Beginning.
Not only the days, so gentle round flowers, and, above,
around the configured trees, so mighty and strong.

Not only the fervour of these unfolded forces,
not only the walks, not only the evening meadows,
not only, after late thunder, the breathing clearness,
not only, evenings, sleep coming and something
        surmised ...
No, but the nights as well! the lofty, the summer
nights, – but the stars as well, the stars of the earth!
Oh, to be dead at last and endlessly know them,
all the stars! For how, how, how to forget them!

Look, I've been calling the lover. But not only she
would come ... Out of unwithholding graves
girls would come and gather ... For how could I limit
the call I had called? The sunken are always seeking
earth again. – You children, I'd say, a single
thing comprehended here's as good as a thousand.
Don't think Destiny's more than what's packed
        into childhood.
How often you'd overtake the beloved, panting,
panting from blissful pursuit of nothing but distance!
Being here's glorious! Even you knew it, you girls.
who went without, as it seemed, sank under, – you,
        in the vilest
streets of cities, festering, or open for refuse.
For to each was granted an hour, – perhaps not quite
so much as an hour – some span that could scarcely
        be measured

by measures of time, in between two whiles,
    when she really
possessed an existence. All. Veins full of existence.
But we so lightly forget what our laughing neighbour
neither confirms nor envies. We want to be visibly
able to show it; whereas the most visible joy
can only reveal itself to us when we've transformed it,
    within.

Nowhere, beloved, can world exist but within.
Life passes in transformation. And, ever diminishing,
outwardness dwindles. Where once was a permanent
    house,
up starts some invented structure across our vision, as fully
at home among concepts as though it still stood in a brain.
Spacious garners of power are formed by the Time Spirit,
    formless
as the high-tensioning urge wrested by him out of all.
Temples he knows no longer. We're now more secretly
    saving
such lavish expenses of heart. Nay, even where one
    survives,
one single thing once prayed or tended or knelt to,
it's started to reach, as it is, into invisibleness.
Many perceive it no more, but neglect the advantage
of building it grandlier now, with pillars and statues,
    within!

* * *

Each torpid turn of the world has such disinherited
     children,
those to whom former has ceased, next hasn't come, to
     belong.
For even the next is far for mankind. Though this
shall not confuse us, shall rather confirm us in keeping
still recognizable form. This *stood* once among
     mankind,
stood in the midst of Fate, the extinguisher, stood
in the midst of not-knowing-whither, as though it
     existed, and bowed
stars from established heavens towards it. Angel,
I'll show it to you as well – there! In your gaze
it shall stand redeemed at last, in a final uprightness.
Pillars, pylons, the Sphinx, all the striving thrust,
greyly from fading or foreign town, of the spire!
Was it not miracle? Angel, gaze, for it's *we* –
O mightiness, tell them that *we* were capable of it –
     my breath's
too short for this celebration. So, after all, we have *not*
failed to make use of the spaces, these generous spaces,
     these,
our spaces. (How terribly big they must be,
when, with thousands of years of our feeling, they're
     not overcrowded.)

But a tower was great, was it not? Oh, Angel, it was,
     though, –
even compared with you? Chartres was great –
    and music
towered still higher and passed beyond us. Why, even
a girl in love, alone, at her window, at night . . .
did she not reach to your knee? –
                       Don't think that I'm wooing!
Angel, even if I were, you'd never come! For my call
is always full of outgoing; against such a powerful
current you cannot advance. Like an outstretched
arm is my call. And its hand, for some grasping,
skywardly opened, remains before you
as opened so wide but for warding
and warning, Inapprehensible.

THE EIGHTH ELEGY
DEDICATED TO RUDOLF KASSNER

With all its eyes the creature-world beholds
the open. But our eyes, as though reversed,
encircle it on every side, like traps
set round its unobstructed path to freedom.
What *is* outside, we know from the brute's face
alone; for while a child's quite small we take it
and turn it round and force it to look backwards
at conformation, not that openness
so deep within the brute's face. Free from death.
We alone see *that*; the free animal
has its decease perpetually behind it
and God in front, and when it moves, it moves
within eternity, like running springs.
We've never, no, not for a single day,
pure space before us, such as that which flowers
endlessly open into: always world,
and never nowhere without no: that pure,
unsuperintended element one breathes,
endlessly knows, and never craves. A child
sometimes gets quietly lost there, to be always
jogged back again. Or someone dies and *is* it.
For, nearing death, one perceives death no longer,
and stares ahead – perhaps with large brute gaze.

Lovers – were not the other present, always
blocking the view! – draw near to it and wonder . . .
Behind the other, as though through oversight,
the thing's revealed . . . But no one gets beyond
the other, and so world returns once more.
Always facing Creation, we perceive there
only a mirroring of the free and open,
dimmed by our breath. Or that a dumb brute's calmly
raising its head to look us through and through.
For this is Destiny: being opposite,
and nothing else, and always opposite.

Did consciousness such as we have exist
in the sure animal that moves towards us
upon a different course, the brute would drag us
round in its wake. But its own being for it
is infinite, inapprehensible,
unintrospective, pure, like its outgazing.
Where we see Future, it sees Everything,
itself in Everything, for ever healed.

And yet, within the wakefully-warm beast
there lies the weight and care of a great sadness.
For that which often overwhelms us clings
to him as well, – a kind of memory
that what one's pressing after now was once

nearer and truer and attached to us
with infinite tenderness. Here all is distance,
there it was breath. Compared with that first home
the second seems ambiguous and fickle.
Oh, bliss of *tiny* creatures that *remain*
for ever in the womb that brought them forth!
Joy of the gnat, that can still leap *within*,
even on its wedding-day: for womb is all!
Look at the half-assurance of the bird,
through origin almost aware of both,
like one of those Etruscan souls, escaped
from a dead man enclosed within a space
on which his resting figure forms a lid.
And how dismayed is any womb-born thing
that has to fly! As though it were afraid
of its own self, it zigzags through the air
like crack through cup. The way a bat's track runs
rendingly through the evening's porcelain.

And we, spectators always, everywhere,
looking at, never out of, everything!
It fills us. We arrange it. It collapses.
We re-arrange it, and collapse ourselves.

Who's turned us round like this, so that we always,
do what we may, retain the attitude

of someone who's departing? Just as he,
on the last hill, that shows him all his valley
for the last time, will turn and stop and linger,
we live our lives, for ever taking leave.

THE NINTH ELEGY

Why, when this span of life might be fleeted away
as laurel, a little darker than all
the surrounding green, with tiny waves on the border
of every leaf (like the smile of a wind): – oh, why
have to be human, and, shunning Destiny,
long for Destiny? . . .

                          Not because happiness really
exists, that precipitate profit of imminent loss.
Not out of curiosity, not just to practise the heart,

that could still be there in laurel. . . .

But because being here is much, and because all this
that's here, so fleeting, seems to require us and
          strangely
concerns us. Us the most fleeting of all. Just once,
everything, only for once. Once and no more. And we, too,
once. And never again. But this
having been once, though only once,
having been once on earth – can it ever be cancelled?

And so we keep pressing on and trying to perform it,
trying to contain it within our simple hands,
in the more and more crowded gaze, in the speechless
          heart.

200

Trying to become it. To give it to whom? We'd rather
hold on to it all for ever ... But into the other relation,
what, alas! do we carry across? Not the beholding
    we've here
slowly acquired, and no here occurrence. Not one.
Sufferings, then. Above all, the hardness of life,
the long experience of love; in fact,
purely untellable things. But later,
under the stars, what use? the more deeply untellable
    stars?
Yet the wanderer too doesn't bring from mountain
    to valley
a handful of earth, of for all untellable earth, but only
a word he has won, pure, the yellow and blue
gentian. Are we, perhaps, *here* just for saying: House,
Bridge, Fountain, Gate, Jug, Fruit tree, Window, –
possibly: Pillar, Tower? ... but for *saying*, remember,
oh, for such saying as never the things themselves
hoped so intensely to be. Is not the secret purpose
of this sly Earth, in urging a pair of lovers,
just to make everything leap with ecstasy in them?
Threshold: what does it mean
to a pair of lovers, that they should be wearing their own
worn threshold a little, they too, after the many before,
before the many to come, ... as a matter of course!

Here is the time for the Tellable, *here* is its home.

Speak and proclaim. More than ever
things we can live with are falling away, for that
which is oustingly taking their place is an imageless act.
Act under crusts, that will readily split as soon
as the doing within outgrows them and takes a
     new outline.
Between the hammers lives on
our heart, as between the teeth
the tongue, which, in spite of all,
still continues to praise.
Praise this world to the Angel, not the untellable: you
can't impress him with the splendour you've felt;
     in the cosmos
where he more feelingly feels you're only a novice.
     So show him
some simple thing, refashioned by age after age,
till it lives in our hands and eyes as a part of ourselves.
Tell him *things*. He'll stand more astonished: as you did
beside the roper in Rome or the potter in Egypt.
Show him how happy a thing can be, how guileless
     and ours;
how even the moaning of grief purely determines on form,
serves as a thing, or dies into a thing, – to escape
to a bliss beyond the fiddle. These things that live on
     departure
understand when you praise them: fleeting, they look for
rescue through something in us, the most fleeting of all.

Want us to change them entirely, within our invisible
        hearts,
into – oh, endlessly – into ourselves! Whosoever we are.

Earth, is it not just this that you want: to arise
invisibly in us? Is not your dream
to be one day invisible? Earth! invisible!
What is your urgent command, if not transformation?
Earth, you darling, I will! Oh, believe me, you need
no more of your spring-times to win me over:
        a single one,
ah, one, is already more than my blood can endure.
Beyond all names I am yours, and have been for ages.
You were always right, and your holiest inspiration
is Death, that friendly Death.
Look, I am living. On what? Neither childhood
        nor future
are growing less. . . . . . Supernumerous existence
wells up in my heart.

THE TENTH ELEGY

Some day, emerging at last out of this fell insight,
may I lift up jubilant praise to assenting Angels!
May not one of the clear-struck keys of the heart
fail to respond through alighting on slack or doubtful
or rending strings! May a brighter radiance stream
     from
my streaming face! May inconspicuous Weeping
flower! How dear you will be to me then, you Nights
of Affliction! Why did I not, inconsolable sisters,
more kneelingly welcome you, more loosenedly
     render
myself to your loosened hair? We wasters of sorrows!
How we stare away into sad endurance beyond them,
trying to foresee their end! Whereas they are nothing
     else
than our winter foliage, our sombre evergreen, *one*
of the seasons of our interior year, – not only
season – they're also place, settlement, camp, soil,
     dwelling.

Strange, though, alas! are the streets of the City
     of Pain,
where, in the pseudo-silence of drowned commotion,
loudly swaggers the casting cast from vacuity's
mould: the begilded ado, the bursting memorial.

How an Angel would trample it down beyond trace,
    their market of comfort,
with the church alongside, bought ready for use: as clean
and disenchanted and shut as the Post on a Sunday!
Outside, though, there's always the billowing edge of
    the fair.
Swings of Freedom! Divers and Jugglers of Zeal!
And the figured shooting-range of bedizened
    Happiness: targets
tumbling in tinny contortions whenever some
    better shot
happens to hit one. Cheer-struck, on he goes reeling
after his luck. For booths that can please
the most curious tastes are drumming and bawling.
    Especially
worth seeing (for adults only): the breeding of Money!
Anatomy made amusing! Money's organs on view!
Nothing concealed! Instructive, and guaranteed to
    increase fertility! . . . .

                   . . . Oh, but then just outside,
behind the last hoarding, plastered with placards for
    'Deathless',
that bitter beer that tastes quite sweet to its drinkers
so long as they chew with it plenty of fresh
    distractions, –
just at the back of the hoardings, just behind them,
    it's real!

Children are playing, and lovers holding each other, – aside,
gravely, in pitiful grass, and dogs are following nature.
The youth is drawn further on; perhaps he's in love with a youthful
Lament . . . He emerges behind her into the meadows, she says:
A long way. We live out there . . . . .

Where ? And the youth
follows. He's touched by her manner. Her shoulder, her neck, – perhaps
she comes of a famous stock? But he leaves her, turns back,
looks round, nods . . . What's the use? She's just a Lament.

Only the youthfully-dead, in their first condition of timeless serenity, that of being weaned,
follow her lovingly. Girls
she awaits and befriends. Gently, she shows them
what she is wearing. Pearls of Pain and the fine-spun
Veils of Endurance. – Youths
she walks with in silence.

But there, where they live, in the valley, one of the elder Laments
takes to the youth when he questions her: – we were once,

she says, a great family, we Lamentations. Our fathers
worked the mines in that mountain-range: among men
you'll find a lump, now and then, of polished original pain,
or of drossy petrified rage from some old volcano.
Yes, that came from there. We used to be rich.

And lightly she leads him on through the spacious
      landscape
of Lamentation, shows him the temple columns,
      the ruins
of towers from which, long ago, Lords of the House
      of Lament
wisely governed the land. Shows him the tall
Tear trees, shows him the fields of flowering Sadness
(only as tender foliage known to the living);
shows him the pasturing herds of Grief, – and, at times,
startled, a bird will draw, flush-flying through their
      uplook,
far into distance the script form of its solitary cry. –
At evening she leads him on to the graves of the
      longest-
lived of the House of Lament, the sibyls and warners.
But, night approaching, they move more gently,
      and soon
moon-like emerges, the all-
guarding sepulchral stone. Twin-brother to that
      on the Nile,

the lofty Sphinx, the taciturn chamber's gaze.
And they start at the regal head that has silently poised,
for ever, the human face
on the scale of the stars.

His sight, still dizzy with early death,
can't take it in. But her gaze
frightens an owl from behind the pschent. And the
     bird,
brushing, in slow down-skimming, along the cheek,
the one with the ripest curve,
faintly inscribes on the new
death-born hearing, as though on the double
page of an opened book, the indescribable outline.

And, higher, the stars. New ones. Stars of the Land
     of Pain.
Slowly she names them: 'There,
look: the *Rider*, the *StaV*, and that fuller constellation
they call *Fruitgarland.* Then, further, towards the Pole:
Cradle, Way, The Burning Book, Doll, Window.
But up in the southern sky, pure as within the palm
of a consecrated hand, the clearly-resplendent *M*,
standing for Mothers. . . . . .'

* * *

But the dead must go on, and, in silence,
    the elder Lament
brings him as far as the gorge
where it gleams in the moonlight, –
there, the source of Joy. With awe
she names it, says 'Among men
it's a carrying stream'.

They stand at the foot of the range.
And there she embraces him, weeping.

Lone he ascends to the mountains of Primal Pain.
And never once does his step sound from the soundless
    fate.

And yet, were they waking a symbol within us, the
    endlessly dead,
look, they'd be pointing, perhaps, to the catkins, hanging
from empty hazels, or else
to the rain downfalling on dark soil-bed in early Spring. –
And we, who think of *ascending*
happiness, then would feel
the emotion that almost startles
when happiness *falls*.

From LETTERS TO A
YOUNG POET

TRANSLATED BY REGINALD SNELL

INTRODUCTION BY THE YOUNG POET

Berlin, June 1929

It was in the late autumn of 1902 – I was sitting in the park of the Military Academy in Wiener-Neustadt, beneath some ancient chestnut trees, and was reading a book. I was so engrossed in reading that I hardly noticed how I was joined by the only non-officer among our professors, the learned and kind-hearted parson of the Academy, Horaček. He took the volume out of my hand, looked at the wrapper and shook his head. 'Poems by Rainer Maria Rilke?' he asked meditatively. He turned over the leaves here and there, glanced through a few verses, gazed thoughtfully into the distance and finally nodded. 'So then the pupil René Rilke has become a poet.'

And I learnt about the thin, pale-faced boy who his parents had sent to the Military *Unterrealschule* in Sankt-Pölten more than fifteen years previously, so that he might later become an officer. At that time Horaček had been employed there as chaplain, and he still remembered his former pupil distinctly. He depicted him as a quiet, solemn, highly capable boy who liked to keep himself apart, bore the restrictions of a boarder's life patiently, and after his fourth year moved on with the others to the Military *Oberrealschule* which was situated in Mährisch-Weisskirchen. There, however, his constitution proved insufficiently resilient, and so his parents removed him from the institution and let him continue his studies at home in Prague. Horaček could report no further on the course which his outward life had thereafter taken.

After all this it may be easily understood that I resolved in that very hour to send my poetical efforts to Rainer Maria Rilke and ask for his opinion. Being not yet twenty years old and barely on the threshold of a profession which I felt to be directly opposed to my inclinations, I hoped to find understanding, if anywhere at all, in the writer of the poems *To Celebrate Myself*. And without my actually having wished it, my verses came to be accompanied by a covering letter in which I revealed myself without reserve as I have never done before or since to another human being.

Many weeks went by before an answer came. The blue-sealed communication bore the post mark of Paris, weighed heavy in the hand and shewed on the envelope the same clear, beautiful and firm characters in which the text was set down from the first line to the last. With that began my regular correspondence with Rainer Maria Rilke, which lasted until 1908 and then gradually trickled into nothing, since life drove me off into regions against which the poet's warm, delicate and touching solicitude had really tried to guard me.

But that is not important. The only thing of impor-
tance is the ten letters which here follow, important
for the appreciation of the world in which Rainer
Maria Rilke lived and worked, and important too for
many who are now growing up and developing, today
and tomorrow. And where a great and unique man
speaks, small men must keep silence.

Franz Xaver Kappus.

I

Paris, February 17th 1903

Dear Sir,

Your letter reached me only a few days ago. I want
to thank you for its great and welcome trust. I can
hardly say more. I cannot go into the quality of your
verses; for I am too far removed from every kind of
critical intention. In making contact with a work of
art nothing serves so ill as words of criticism: the
invariable result is more or less happy misunderstand-
ings. Things are not all so comprehensible and utter-
able as people would mostly have us believe; most
events are unutterable, consummating themselves in a
sphere where word has never trod, and more unutter-
able than them all are works of art, whose life endures
by the side of our own that passes away.

Having written this note by way of introduction, may I just go on to tell you that your verses have no individual quality, but rather, quiet and hidden tendencies to something personal. I feel this most clearly in the last poem *My Soul*. And in the beautiful poem *To Leopardi* there is perhaps growing up a kind of relationship with that great and solitary man. All the same, the poems are not yet anything in themselves, nothing independent, not even the last one or the one to Leopardi. Your friendly letter which accompanied them did not fail to explain to me a number of deficiencies which I felt in reading your verses, without however being able to give a name to them.

You ask if your verses are good. You ask me. You have previously asked others. You send them to journals. You compare them with other poems, and you are troubled when certain editors reject your efforts. Now (as you have permitted me to advise you) I beg you to give all that up. You are looking outwards, and of all things that is what you must now not do. Nobody can advise and help you, nobody. There is only one single means. Go inside yourself. Discover the motive that bids you write; examine whether it sends its roots down to the deepest places of your heart, confess to yourself whether you would have to die if writing were denied you. This before all: ask yourself in the quietest hour of your night: *must* I write? Dig down into yourself for a deep answer. And if this should be in the affirmative, if you may meet this solemn question with a strong and simple *'I must'*, then build your life according to this necessity; your life must, right to its most unimportant and insignificant hour, become a token and a witness of this impulse. Then draw near to Nature. Then try, as if you were one of the first men, to say what you see and experience and love and lose. Do not write love poems; avoid at first those forms which are too familiar and usual: they are the most difficult, for great and fully matured strength is needed to make an individual contribution where good and in part brilliant traditions exist in plenty. Turn therefore from the common themes to those which your own everyday life affords; depict your sorrows and desires, your passing thoughts and belief in some kind of beauty – depict all that with heartfelt, quiet, humble sincerity and use to express yourself the things that surround you, the images of your dreams and the objects of your memory. If your everyday life seems poor to you, do not accuse it; accuse yourself, tell yourself you are not poet enough to summon up its riches; since for the creator there is no poverty and no poor or unimportant place. And even if you were in a prison whose walls allowed none of the sounds of the world to reach your senses –

would you not still have always your childhood, that precious, royal richness, that treasure house of memories? Turn your attention there. Try to raise the submerged sensations of that distant past; your personality will grow stronger, your solitude will extend itself and will become a twilit dwelling which the noise of others passes by in the distance. – And if from this turning inwards, from this sinking into your private world, there come verses, you will not think to ask anyone whether they are good verses. You will not attempt, either, to interest journals in these works: for you will see in them your own dear genuine possession, a portion and a voice of your life. A work of art is good if it has grown out of necessity. In this manner of its origin lies its true estimate: there is no other. Therefore, my dear Sir, I could give you no advice but this: to go into yourself and to explore the depths whence your life wells forth; at its source you will find the answer to the question whether you *must* create. Accept it as it sounds, without enquiring too closely into every word. Perhaps it will turn out that you are called to be an artist. Then take your fate upon yourself and bear it, its burden and its greatness, without ever asking for that reward which might come from without. For the creator must be a world for himself, and find everything within himself, and in Nature to which he has attached himself.

Perhaps however, after this descent into yourself and into your aloneness, you will have to renounce your claim to become a poet; (it is sufficient, as I have said, to feel that one could live without writing, in order not to venture it at all.) But even then this introversion which I beg of you has not been in vain. Your life will at all events find thenceforward its individual paths; and that they may be good and rich and far reaching I wish for you more than I can say.

What more shall I say to you? Everything seems to me to have its proper emphasis; I would finally just like to advise you to grow through your development quietly and seriously; you can interrupt it in no more violent manner than by looking outwards, and expecting answer from outside to questions which perhaps only your innermost feeling in your most silent hour can answer....

With every respect and sympathy:
Rainer Maria Rilke.

II

Viareggio near Pisa (Italy), April 5th 1903

... I wanted to say two further things to you today: irony:

Do not let yourself be governed by it, especially not

in unproductive moments. In productive ones try to make use of it as one more means of seizing life. Used purely, it is itself pure, and one need not be ashamed of it; and when you feel too familiar with it, when you fear the growing intimacy with it, then turn towards great and serious subjects, before which it becomes small and helpless. Seek for the depth of things: there irony never descends – and when you have thus brought it to the edge of greatness, test at the same time whether this mode of perception springs from a necessity of your being. For under the influence of serious things it will either fall away from you (if it is something non-essential), or else it will (if it belongs to you innately) with gathering strength become a serious tool and be ranked among the means by which you will have to form your art.

And the second thing that I wanted to tell you today is this:

Only a few of all my books are indispensable to me, and two of these are actually always among my things wherever I am. Even here they are round me: the Bible, and the books of the great Danish writer Jens Peter Jacobsen. It occurs to me to wonder whether you know his works. You can easily procure them, for a part of them has appeared in Reclam's Universal Library in a very good translation. Get hold of the little volume called *Six Tales* by J. P. Jacobsen, and his novel *Niels Lyhne*, and start with the first story in the former book, which is called *Mogens*. A world will come over to you, the happiness, the wealth, the inconceivable greatness of a world. Live for a while in these books, learn from them what seems to you worth learning, but above all love them. Your love will be repaid a thousand thousandfold, and whatever your life may become – will, I am convinced, run through the texture of your growing as one of the most important threads among all the threads of your experiences, disappointments and joys.

If I am to say from whom I have learnt anything about the nature of creation, about its depth and everlastingness, there are only two names that I can mention: Jacobsen, that great, great writer, and Auguste Rodin, who has not his peer among all the artists who are alive today.

And may all success attend your ways!

Yours:

Rainer Maria Rilke.

III

Viareggio near Pisa (Italy), April 23rd 1903

... Your opinion of *There should have been roses there* ... (that work of such incomparable delicacy and form) is of course, in contrast with that expressed in the introduction, quite, quite unimpeachably correct. And let me here at once request you: read as few aesthetic-critical things as possible – they are either partisan opinions, become hardened and meaningless in their lifeless petrification, or else they are a skilful play upon words, in which one view is uppermost today and its opposite tomorrow. Works of art are of an infinite solitariness, and nothing is less likely to bring us near to them than criticism. Only love can apprehend and hold them, and can be just towards them. – Decide each time according to *yourself* and your feelings in the face of every such declaration, discussion or introduction; if you should still be wrong, the natural growth of your inner life will lead you slowly in the course of time to other perceptions. Let your judgements have their own quiet, undisturbed development, which must, like all progress, come from deep within, and cannot in any way be pressed or hurried. It means everything to carry for the full time and then to bring forth. To allow every impression and every germ of a feeling to grow to completion wholly in yourself, in the darkness, in the unutterable, unconscious, inaccessible to your own understanding, and to await with deep humility and patience the hour of birth of a new clarity: that is alone what living as an artist means: in understanding as in creation.

There is no measuring by time there, a year there has no meaning, and ten years are nothing. To be an artist means: not to reckon and count; to ripen like the tree which does not force its sap and stands confident in the storms of Spring without fear lest no Summer might come after. It does come. But it comes only to the patient ones, who are there as if eternity lay in front of them, so unconcernedly still and far. I am learning it daily, learning it through pains to which I am grateful: patience is all!...

Yours:

Rainer Maria Rilke.

IV

Temporarily at Worpswede near Bremen, July 16th 1903

I left Paris about ten days ago, badly ailing and tired, and came to a great northern plain, whose remoteness and silence and sky are to make me well again. But I ran into a long spell of rain, which has only today begun to clear a little over the restlessly waving land; and I am using this first moment of brightness to send you, dear Sir, my greetings.

My dear Herr Kappus: I have left a letter of yours long unanswered, not that I had forgotten it – on the contrary: it was of the kind that one reads again when one finds it among other letters, and I recognized you in it as if you were close at hand. It was the letter of May 2nd, and you doubtless remember it. When I read it, as I do now, in the great stillness of this faraway place, your beautiful concern for life moves me even more than I experienced it in Paris, where everything has a different ring and dies away by reason of the monstrous noise that makes all things tremble. Here, where a vast countryside is around me, over which the winds come in from the seas, here I feel that there is nowhere a human being who can answer you those questions and feelings which have a life of their own within their depths; for even the best men go astray with words, when these are to express something very gentle and almost unutterable. But I believe nevertheless that you need not be left without some solution, if you hold to things similar to those on which my eyes now take their recreation. If you hold to Nature, to the simplicity that is in her, to the small detail that scarcely one man sees, which can so unexpectedly grow into something great and boundless; if you have this love for insignificant things and seek, simply as one who serves, to win the confidence of what seems to be poor: then everything will become easier for you, more coherent and somehow more conciliatory, not perhaps in the understanding, which lags wondering behind, but in your innermost consciousness, wakefulness and knowing. You are so young, you have not even begun, and I would like to beg you, dear Sir, as well as I can, to have patience with everything that is unsolved in your heart and to try to cherish the questions themselves, like closed rooms and like books written in a very strange tongue. Do not search now for the answers which cannot be given you because you could not live them. It is a matter of living everything. Live the questions now. Perhaps you will then gradually, without noticing it, one distant day live right into the answer. Perhaps indeed you carry within yourself the possibility of shaping and forming, as a particularly pure and blessed kind of life; train yourself for it – but take what comes in complete trust, if only it comes from your will, from some inner need of yours, take it to yourself and do not hate anything. Sex is difficult; yes. But it is the difficult that is enjoined upon us, almost everything serious is difficult, and everything is serious. If you only recognize that and contrive, yourself, out of your own disposition and nature, out of your experience and childhood and strength to achieve an entirely individual relationship to sex (not influenced by convention and custom), then you need no longer fear to lose yourself and become unworthy of your best possession.

Bodily delight is a sense of experience, just like pure

seeing or the pure feeling with which a lovely fruit fills the tongue; it is a great boundless experience which is given us, a knowing of the world, the fullness and the splendour of all knowing. Our acceptance of it is not bad; what is bad is that almost all men misuse and squander this experience, and apply it as a stimulus to the weary places of their life, a dissipation instead of a rallying for the heights. Mankind have turned eating, too, into something else: want on the one hand, and superfluity on the other, have dulled the clarity of this need, and all those deep, simple necessities by which life renews itself have become similarly dull. But the individual can clarify them for himself and live clearly, (or if not the individual, who is too dependent, then at any rate the solitary man.) He can remember that all beauty in animals and plants is a quiet enduring form of love and longing, and he can see the animal, as he sees the plant, patiently and willingly uniting and propagating itself and growing, not from physical lust, not from physical pain, but bowing to necessities which are greater than lust and pain and more powerful than will and opposition. O that man might be more humble in accepting this secret of which the earth is full even in its tiniest creatures, and more sincere in bearing, enduring and feeling how frightfully serious it is, instead of taking it lightly. That he might be reverent towards his fertility, which is all one whether it be intellectual or physical; for intellectual creation too derives from the physical, is of one substance with it, it is only like a gentler, more enraptured and everlasting repetition of bodily delight. 'The thought of being a creator, of begetting and forming' is nothing without its continual great confirmation and realization in the world, nothing without the thousandfold assent from things and animals – and its enjoyment is so indescribably beautiful and rich only because it is full of inherited memories of the begetting and bearing of millions. In one creator's thought a thousand forgotten nights of love revive again and fill it full of loftiness and grandeur. Those who come together in the night time and entwine in swaying delight perform a serious work and gather up sweetness, depth and strength for the song of some poet that is to be, who will rise to tell of unspeakable bliss. And they summon the future; and even though they go astray and embrace blindly, yet the future comes, a new human being arises, and on the basis of the chance occurrence which here seems consummated, awakens the law by which a resistant vigorous seed forces its way to the egg-cell that advances openly to meet it. Do not let yourself be misled by outward appearances; in the depths everything becomes law. And those who live the secret falsely and badly (and they are very many) only lose it for themselves and yet hand it on like a sealed letter, without knowing it. And do not be confused by the multiplicity of names and the complexity of instances. Perhaps there is over everything a great motherhood, as a common longing. The loveliness of the virgin, a being that (as you so beautifully say) 'has not yet accomplished anything', is motherhood foreboding and preparing itself, uneasy and yearning. And the mother's beauty is serving motherhood, and in the old woman there is a great memory. And in the man too there is motherhood, it seems to me, physical and spiritual; his begetting is also a kind of birth-giving, and it is birth-giving when he creates out of his innermost fullness. And perhaps the sexes are more akin than we suppose, and the great renewal of the world will perhaps consist in this, that man and maiden, freed from all false feelings and perversions, will seek each other not as opposites but as brother and sister, as neighbours, and will unite as human beings to bear in common, simply, seriously and patiently, the heavy sex that has been laid upon them.

But everything that once perhaps will be possible to many, the solitary man can already prepare for and build now with his hands, which go less astray. Therefore, dear Sir, love your solitude and bear the pain which it has caused you with fair-sounding lament. For those that are near you are far, you say, and this shews that distance begins to grow round you. And when your nearness is far, then your distance is already among the stars and very great; be glad of your growing, into which you can take no one else with you, and be good to those that remain behind, and be self-possessed and quiet with them and do not torment them with your doubts and do not frighten them with your confidence or joy, which they could not comprehend. Seek some unpretending and honest communication with them, which you are under no necessity to alter when you yourself become more and more different; love life in a strange guise in them, and make allowances for those ageing people who fear the solitude in which you trust. Avoid furnishing material for a drama which is always impending between parents and children; it uses up much of the children's strength and wastes away the love of their elders, which is operative and warm even when it does not comprehend. Demand no advice from them and reckon with no understanding; but believe in a love that is preserved for you like a heritage, and trust that in this love there is a strength and a blessing which you are not bound to leave behind you though you may travel far!

It is good that you are entering first of all upon a profession which makes you independent and places you on your own in every sense. Wait patiently to see whether your innermost life feels constrained by the form of this profession. I consider it a very difficult one and a hard taskmaster, as it is burdened with much convention and gives hardly any scope to a personal interpretation of its tasks. But your solitude will be your home and haven even in the midst of very strange conditions, and from there you will discover all your paths. All my wishes are ready to accompany you, and my trust is with you.

Yours:

Rainer Maria Rilke.

VII

Rome, May 14th 1904

... To love is also good: for love is difficult. Fondness between human beings: that is perhaps the most difficult task that is set us, the ultimate thing, the final trial and test, the work for which all other work is only preparation. Therefore young people, who are beginners in everything, *cannot* know love yet: they have to learn it. With their whole being, with all their strength gathered about their lonely, fearful, upward beating heart, they must learn to love. But apprenticeship is always a long, secluded time, and therefore loving is for a long while, far into life −: solitude, heightened and deepened aloneness for him who loves. Loving in the first instance is nothing that can be called losing, surrendering and uniting oneself to another (what would a union be, of something unclarified and unready, still inferior – ?), it is a sublime occasion for the individual to mature, to grow into something in himself, to become world for himself for another's sake, it is a great exacting claim upon him, something that chooses him and summons him to a distant goal. Only in this sense, as a task to work upon themselves ('to hearken and to hammer day and night') might young people use the love that is given them. The self-losing and the surrender and all manner of communion is not for them (they must save and treasure for a long, long while yet), it is the ultimate thing, it is perhaps something for which human lives are so far hardly adequate.

But that is where young people so often and so grievously go wrong: that they (whose nature it is to have no patience) throw themselves at each other when love comes over them, scatter themselves abroad, just as they are in all their untidiness, disorder and confusion . . . : But what is to be done then? How is life to act upon this heap of half crushed matter which they call their communion and which they would dearly like to style their happiness, if that were possible, and their future? So each one loses himself for the other's sake, and loses the other and many others who wanted still to come. And loses the expanses and possibilities, exchanges the drawing near and fleeting away of gentle, presageful things for a sterile helplessness out of which nothing more can come; nothing but a little disgust, disillusion and poverty and delivererance into one of the many conventions which are set up in large numbers as public refuges along this most dangerous of roads. No region of human experience is so well supplied with conventions as this: life-belts of the most varied invention, boats and swimming-bladders are there; social perception has contrived to create shelters of every description, for as it was disposed to take love-life as a pleasure, it had to mould it into something easy, cheap, innocuous and safe, as public pleasures are.

Many young people, to be sure, who love falsely, that is simply surrendering, letting solitude go (the average person will always persist in that way), feel the oppression of failure and want to make the situation in which they find themselves full of vitality and fruitful in their own personal fashion – ; for their nature tells them that even less than anything else of importance can the questions of love be resolved publicly and by this or that compromise; that they are questions, intimate questions from one human being to another, which need in every instance a new, particular, purely personal answer –: but how should those who have already confounded themselves and are no longer bounded or separate, who therefore no longer possess anything individual, be able to find a way out of themselves, out of the depth of their already shattered solitude?

They act out of mutual helplessness, and if then they want, with the best of intentions, to avoid the convention that catches their eye (say that of marriage), they end up in the clutches of a less clamorous but equally deadly conventional solution; for there everything all round them is – convention; where it is a question of a hastily fused, turbid communion, every possible action must be conventional; every relationship to which such entanglement leads has its convention, be it as unusual as it may (that is, in the ordinary sense immoral); why, even separation would in such a case be a conventional step, an impersonal random decision without strength and without effect.

Anyone who considers it seriously will find that for difficult love, as for death, which is difficult, no explanation, no solution, neither sign nor path has yet been made known; and for both these tasks which we carry secretly and hand on without uncovering them, no universal rule based on agreed principles can be discovered. But in proportion as we begin to make individual trial of life, these great things will meet us as individuals at closer quarters. The claims which the difficult work of love lays upon our development are more than life-sized, and as beginners we are not equal to them. But if we continue to hold out and take this love upon ourselves as a burden and apprenticeship, instead of losing ourselves in all the light and frivolous play behind which mankind have concealed themselves from the most serious gravity of their existence – then perhaps some small progress and some alleviation will become perceptible to those who come long after us; that would be much.

We are really only just beginning to regard the relationship of a human individual to another individual dispassionately and objectively, and our attempts to live such a relationship have no pattern before them. And yet in the passage of time there are now several things that are ready to help our shy novitiate.

The girl and the woman in their new, individual unfolding will be only transient imitators of bad or good masculine behaviour, and repeaters of masculine professions. After the uncertainty of such transitions it will be seen that women have passed through the exuberance and vicissitudes of those (often ridiculous) disguises, only in order to purify their most essential being from the distorting influence of the other sex. Surely women, in whom life tarries and dwells more immediately, fruitfully and confidently, must have become fundamentally more mature human beings, more *human* human beings, than light man, whom the weight of no body's fruit pulls down beneath the surface of life, who, conceited and rash as he is, underrates what he thinks he loves. The humanity of woman, brought forth in pains and degradations, will come to light when she has shed the conventions of mere femininity in the alterations of her outward station, and the men who today do not feel it coming will be surprised and struck by it. One day (for this there are already reliable signs speaking and shining, especially in the northern countries), one day the girl will be here and the woman whose name will no longer signify merely the opposite of masculinity, but something in itself, something which makes us think of no complement or limitation, but only of life and existence – : the feminine human being.

This step forward will (very much against the wishes of outstripped man to begin with) change the love experience that now is full of error, alter it fundamentally, refashion it into a relationship meant to be between one human being and another no longer between man and wife. And this more human love (which will consummate itself infinitely thoughtfully and gently, and well and clearly in binding and loosing) will be something like that which we are preparing with struggle and toil, the love which consists in the mutual guarding, bordering and saluting of two solitudes.

And one thing more: do not think that the great love which was once enjoined upon you as a boy, became lost; can you say whether great and good wishes were not then ripening within you, and resolutions by which you live to this day? I believe that this love remains so strong and powerful in your memory because it was your first deep aloneness and the first inner work which you did upon your life. – All good wishes for you, dear Herr Kappus!

Yours:

Rainer Maria Rilke.

VIII

Borgeby Gård, Flädie, Sweden, August 12th 1904

... I believe that almost all our sorrows are moments of tension which we experience as paralysis, because we no longer hear our estranged feelings living. Because we are alone with the strange thing that has entered into us; because for a moment everything familiar and customary has been taken from us; because we stand in the middle of a crossing where we cannot remain standing. Therefore it is, also, that the sorrow passes by us: the new thing in us, that has been added to us, has entered into our heart, has gone into its innermost chamber, and is no more even there – is already in the blood. And we do not realize what it was. We could easily be made to believe that nothing had happened, and yet we have been changed, as a house is changed into which a guest has entered. We cannot say who has come, perhaps we shall never know, but there are many indications to suggest that the future is entering into us in this manner in order to transform itself within us long before it happens. And therefore it is so important to be solitary and heedful when we are sad: because the seemingly uneventful and inflexible moment when our future sets foot in us stands so much nearer to life than that other noisy and fortuitous instant when it happens to us as if from without. The more patient, quiet and open we are in our sorrowing, the more deeply and the more unhesitatingly will the new thing enter us, the better shall we deserve it, the more will it be our own destiny, and when one day later it 'happens' (that is, goes forth from us to others) we shall feel in our inmost selves that we are akin and close to it. And that is necessary. It is necessary – and in that direction our development will gradually move – that nothing alien shall befall us, but only what has long been part of us. We have already had to think anew so many concepts of motion, we shall also learn gradually to realize that it is out of mankind that what we call destiny proceeds, not into them from without. Only because so many did not absorb their destinies and transform these within themselves as long as they lived in them, they did not recognize what went forth from them; it was so alien to them that they believed, in their bewildered terror, it must have just entered into them, for they swore that they had never before found anything similar in themselves. As we have long deceived ourselves about the motion of the sun, so we still continue to deceive ourselves about the motion of that which is to come. The future stands firm, dear Herr Kappus, but we move about in infinite space.

How should we not find it difficult?

And, to speak again of solitude, it becomes increasingly clear that this is fundamentally not something that we can choose or reject. We *are* solitary. We can delude ourselves about it, and pretend that it is not so. That is all. But how much better it is to realize that we are thus, to start directly from that very point. Then, to be sure, it will come about that we grow dizzy; for all the points upon which our eyes have been accustomed to rest will be taken away from us, there is no longer any nearness, and all distance is infinitely far. A man who was taken from his study, almost without preparation and transition, and placed upon the height of a great mountain range, would be bound to feel something similar: an uncertainty without parallel, an abandonment to the unutterable would almost annihilate him. He would imagine himself to be falling or fancy himself flung outwards into space or exploded into a thousand pieces: what a monstrous lie his brain would have to invent in order to retrieve and explain the condition of his senses. So all distances, all measures are changed for the man who becomes solitary; many of these changes take effect suddenly, and, as with the man on the mountain top, there arise singular fantasies and strange sensations which seem to grow out beyond all endurance. But it is necessary for us to experience that too. We must accept our existence as far as ever it is possible; everything, even the unheard of, must be possible there. That is fundamentally the only courage which is demanded of us: to be brave in the face of the strangest, most singular and most inexplicable things that can befall us. The fact that human beings have been cowardly in this sense has done endless harm to life; the experiences that are called 'apparitions', the whole of the so-called 'spirit world', death, all these things that are so closely related to us, have been so crowded out of life by our daily warding them off, that the senses by which we might apprehend them are stunted. To say nothing of God. But fear of the inexplicable has not only impoverished the existence of the solitary man, it has also circumscribed the relationships between human beings, as it were lifted them up from the river bed of infinite possibilities to a fallow spot on the bank, to which nothing happens. For it is not only indolence which causes human relationships to repeat themselves with such unspeakable monotony, unrenewed from one occasion to another, it is the shyness of any new, incalculable experience which we do not feel ourselves equal to facing. But only the man who is prepared for everything, who excludes nothing, not even the most unintelligible, will live the relationship with another as something vital, and will himself exhaust his own existence. For if we think of this existence of the individual as a larger or smaller room, it becomes clear that most people get to know only one corner of their room, a window seat, a strip of floor which they pace up and down. In that way they have a certain security. And yet how much more human is that insecurity, so fraught with danger, which compels the prisoners in Poe's Tales to grope for the shapes of their ghastly prisons and not to remain unaware of the unspeakable horrors of their dwelling. But we are not prisoners. No snares and springes are laid for us, and there is nothing that should alarm or torment us. We are set in life as in the element with which we are most in keeping, and we have moreover, through thousands of years of adaptation, become so similar to this life that when we stay still we are, by a happy mimicry, hardly to be distinguished from our surroundings. We have no cause to be mistrustful of our world, for it is not against us. If it has terrors they are our terrors; if it has abysses those abysses belong to us, if dangers are there we must strive to love them. And if only we regulate our life according to that principle which advises us always to hold to the difficult, what even now appears most alien to us will become most familiar and loyal. How could we forget those old myths which are to be found in the beginnings of every people; the myths of the dragons which are transformed, at the last moment, into princesses; perhaps all the dragons of our life are princesses, who are only waiting to see us once beautiful and brave. Perhaps everything terrifying is at bottom the helplessness that seeks our help.

So you must not be frightened, dear Herr Kappus, when a sorrow rises up before you, greater than you have ever seen before; when a restlessness like light and cloud shadows passes over your hands and over all your doing. You must think that something is happening upon you, that life has not forgotten you, that it holds you in its hand; it will not let you fall. Why do you want to exclude any disturbance, any pain, any melancholy from your life, since you do not know what these conditions are working upon you? Why do you want to plague yourself with the question where it has all come from and whither it is tending? Since you know that you are in a state of transition and would wish nothing so dearly as to transform yourself. If something in your proceedings is diseased, do reflect that disease is the means by which an organism rids itself of a foreign body; you must then simply help it to be ill, to have its full disease and to let it break out, for that is its development. In you, dear Herr Kappus, so much is happening now; you must be patient like a sick man and sanguine like a convalescent; for perhaps you are both. And more than that: you are also the doctor who has to superintend yourself. But in every illness there are many days when the doctor can do nothing but wait. And that is what you, in so far as you are your own doctor, must now above all things do.

Do not observe yourself too closely. Do not draw too rapid conclusions from what happens to you; let it simply happen to you. Otherwise you will too easily reach the point of looking reproachfully (that is morally) at your past, which is naturally concerned with everything that is now occurring to you. But what is taking effect in you from the mistakes, desires and longings of your boyhood is not what you recall and condemn. The extraordinary circumstances of a solitary and helpless childhood are so difficult, so complicated, exposed to so many influences and at the same time so untrammelled by all real connection with life, that where a vice appears in it we must not call it a vice and leave it at that. One must in general be so careful with names; it is so often the name of a misdeed upon which a life is shattered, not the nameless and personal action itself, which was perhaps a quite definite necessity of that life and could be taken on by it without trouble. And the expense of energy seems to you so great only because you overrate the victory; this latter is not the 'great thing' that you think you have achieved, although you are right about your feelings; the great thing is that something was already there which you could set in place of that betrayal, something true and genuine. Apart from this even your victory would have been only a moral reaction without great significance, but thus it has become a chapter of your life. Of your life, dear Herr Kappus, about which I am thinking with so many wishes. Do you remember how this life has longed ever since childhood for the 'great'? I see how it is now longing to leave the great for greater. Therefore it does not cease to be difficult, but therefore it will not cease, either, to grow.

And if I may say one thing more to you, it is this:

do not think that the man who seeks to comfort you lives untroubled among the simple and quiet words which sometimes do you good. His life has much hardship and sadness and lags far behind them. If it were otherwise, he could never have found those words.

Yours:

Rainer Maria Rilke.

X

Paris, the second day of Christmas 1908

You must know, dear Herr Kappus, how glad I was to have that beautiful letter from you. The news which you give me, real and expressible as it now again is, seems to me good, and the longer I have considered it, the more I have felt that it is in actual fact good. I really wanted to write this to you for Christmas Eve; but with all the work in which I have been variously and unremittingly living this winter, the festival has come upon me so quickly that I have hardly had any time over to see to my most necessary business, much less to write.

But I have thought of you often during these festival days, and imagined how quiet you must be in your lonely fort among the empty mountains, over which those great southerly winds are pouring themselves as if they wanted to devour them in great lumps.

The stillness must be immense in which such sounds and movements have room, and when one considers that to all these is added at the same time the resounding presence of the distant sea, perhaps as the innermost voice in this prehistoric harmony, one can only wish for you that you may confidently and patiently let that sublime solitude work upon you, which can no more be expunged from your life; which will work continuously and with gentle decision as an anonymous influence in everything that lies before you, somewhat as ancestral blood moves incessantly within us and mingles with our own to form that unique and unrepeatable compound that we are at every turning of our life.

Yes: I am glad that you have this steady expressible existence with you, this title, this uniform, this duty, all this which is palpable and defined, which in such surroundings with a similarly isolated, not numerous body of men assumes gravity and necessity, betokens a vigilant employment over and above that element of playing and passing the time in the military profession, and not only admits but positively trains an independent alertness. And that we are in circumstances which work upon us, which set us free from time to time to face things that are great and natural, is all that is necessary.

Art too is only a way of living, and one can prepare

for it, living somehow, without knowing it; in every-thing real one is a closer, nearer neighbour to it than in the unreal semi-artistic professions which, while they make show of a relatedness to art, in practice deny and attack the existence of all art, as for instance the whole of journalism does, and almost all criticism and three-quarters of what calls itself and likes to be called literature. I am glad, in a word, that you have overcome the danger of ending up there, and remain solitary and courageous somewhere in a raw reality. May the year that lies before you preserve and strengthen you in that.

Ever yours;

R. M. Rilke.

R.M.R.

4 December 1875–29 December 1926

ROSE, OH THE PURE CONTRADICTION,
DELIGHT, OF BEING NO ONE'S SLEEP
UNDER SO MANY LIDS.

INDEX OF FIRST LINES

250